SAGE CONTEMPORARY SOCIAL SCIENCE ISSUES 1

SOCIOLOGY

OF

LEISURE

Edited by

Theodore B. Johannis Jr.

and

C. Neil Bull

 SAGE PUBLICATIONS *Beverly Hills / London*

PUBLISHER'S NOTE

The material in this publication originally appeared as a special issue of PACIFIC SOCIOLOGICAL REVIEW (Volume 14, Number 3, July 1971). The Publisher would like to acknowledge the assistance of the Pacific Sociological Association and the two special issue editors, Theodore B. Johannis, Jr. and C. Neil Bull, in making this edition possible.

For information address:

SAGE PUBLICATIONS, INC.
275 South Beverly Drive
Beverly Hills, California 90212

SAGE PUBLICATIONS LTD
St George's House / 44 Hatton Garden
London EC1N 8ER

Printed in the United States of America

International Standard Book Number 0-8039-0318-9

Library of Congress Catalog Card No. 73-87853

FIRST PRINTING (this edition)

CONTENTS

From the Editors

In our call for papers for this special issue devoted to the sociology of leisure, we recommended that contributors focus their articles around three aspects of the topic under study: (1) a systematic review of the research and writing which led up to their current research; (2) a presentation of the results of their most recent work; and (3) implications of their thinking and research for the next steps in the analysis of the sociology of leisure. Our purpose in making these recommendations was to attempt to ensure that this issue would not only be devoted to the presentation of some of the latest research on leisure but would make more readily available some of the central topics on which research concerned with leisure might well focus in the future.

The initial response to our request for papers was substantial, thus indicating considerable interest among sociologists in the sociology of leisure. However, the editors were disappointed in the general quality of the manuscripts they received. A few were but reruns of work previously published elsewhere. Several were speculative conceptual schemas void of any substantive attempt to test the proposed "model." The majority were research proposals based upon previously published data or upon casual observation. And, finally, only a few were concerned with ongoing research as per our recommendation. Examination of the outlines for proposed articles and the manuscripts received lead the editors to draw the following conclusions: (1) there does not appear to be an overwhelming

[5]

amount of solid leisure research in progress; (2) a substantial amount of effort is being devoted to the development of conceptual schema which appear to go untested; (3) the attempt to relate the sociology of leisure to the central theoretical and methodological concerns of contemporary sociology is embryonic; (4) descriptive rather than analytic studies are the vogue; and (5) indicating where future research is likely to be most fruitful is a task few contributors are prepared to face. The editors, therefore, selected for inclusion in this special issue articles which cover at least some of the main areas outlined in the first paragraph above, with preference being given to those which concern themselves with ongoing research.

We have singled out several articles for special comment. The article which most nearly fits the proposed focus of this issue is that of Neil H. Cheek, who includes a discussion of future research on the sociology of leisure which he envisions to be most fruitful. While most of the research articles depend upon some form of questionnaire for obtaining the data, the one exception, using participant observation over a considerable period of time, was written by Jo M. Senters. The article by John Neulinger is an example of data from a long-range research program concerned with leisure and offers a different type of contrast. Finally, three articles—those of Cheek, Kando and Summers, and Phillips and Schafer—would seem to be working toward a similar approach to the study of nonwork activities. We hope the readers will find a comparison of these articles useful.

The editors had expected to be able to include a directory of sociologists working in the area of leisure, sports, and the arts. However, due to space limitations and the size of the list, this was not feasible. Copies of the directory may be purchased through Allan H. Ingham, Department of Sociology, University of Massachusetts, Amherst, Mass. 01002.

—Theodore B. Johannis, Jr.
—C. Neil Bull
University of Oregon

TOWARD A SOCIOLOGY OF NOT-WORK

NEIL H. CHEEK, Jr.
National Park Service
U.S. Department of the Interior

The study of leisure has not yet found a firm foothold among American sociologists." With this statement, Rolf Meyersohn (1969: 53) begins a recent article on the sociology of leisure in the United States. If we accept his statement, we must begin to ponder why such a state of affairs should exist. Meyersohn himself considers the question, but does not answer except by inference. For example, he cites an observation made by Bennett Berger a decade ago that "the sociology of leisure today is little else than a reporting of survey data on what selected samples of individuals do with the time in which they are not working and the correlation of these data with conventional demographic variables" (Meyersohn, 1969: 53). Meyersohn agrees with Berger and observes further that "little of the empirical work carried out by sociologists comes close to testing illuminating hypotheses" (1969: 53). Indeed, as he notes later in the same article, "the discovery of correlations of participation in particular leisure activities with social class or occupation are perhaps more valuable to our understanding of the meaning of class than they are toward our understanding of the meaning of leisure" (1969: 57).

One suspects that the same can be said about other variables in addition to those of social class and occupation and their relationships with leisure. Apparently, as Meyersohn and others suggest, sociologists have yet to formulate hypotheses in a manner conducive to developing knowledge about leisure as a sociological entity per se, instead of further verifying the explanatory limits of variables like social class. This paper will explore one possible explanation for this dilemma and suggest a means for establishing studies on a different theoretical basis.

THEORETICAL ORIENTATIONS OF LEISURE STUDIES

To assist the exposition, let us briefly characterize several of the major theoretical orientations found among studies of leisure and recreation. These will necessarily be brief and oversimplified, but will hopefully aid the recall of such arguments.

First, there are studies which attempt to describe how certain leisure activities are associated with the occupations of the individuals in the sample or other indicators of the impact of the economic institutions of a society upon the sociability of its members (Bishop and Ikeda, 1970). These studies usually report summary statements of the general form:

'Activity A is related to condition X.'

Ordinarily, data are obtained from some population through a sample of social persons. As Meyersohn indicates in his bibliography, these are the major proportion of the studies forming the corpus of the sociology of leisure.

Second, there are studies which attempt to assess the validity of the hypothesis that individuals seek activities in their leisure time which are congruent with other aspects of their lives. Thus the older person, presumably as a consequence of aging, engages in gardening as an outdoor activity instead of vigorous hiking. The converse of this hypothesis has also been examined, where individuals are thought to seek activities during leisure time which are quite divergent from other aspects of their lives, particularly their occupational demands (Havighurst, 1957). These studies report findings in the general statement format:

'The greater activity A is like aspect I, the greater the probability that individual (z) will select it instead of activity B.'

Data are usually obtained from individuals and indicate that the object of study is the operation of individual choice and occasionally the reduction of cognitive dissonance.

Third, there are studies in which leisure and play are interpreted as necessary conditions for the physical, mental, and social well-being of the individual. Some of these studies recognize that the everyday world of most individuals is divided between work and leisure and have sought answers to questions about the comparative balance of these two social forces for the individual and some of the problems it presents for a society (DeGrazia, 1962). These studies report their findings in two general statement formats:

'Activity A is a necessary condition for state (x) of the individual to appear and persist.'

'A balance between condition (a) and condition (b) is necessary for the society to persist, i.e., "remain healthy."'

The object of study is the individual as a skin-bounded organism or as a psychological entity.

Finally, there are studies of leisure which take a philosophical perspective and seek the character-building potential for individuals of various recreational activities (Weiss, 1969). Findings are reported in the general statement format:

'Activity A is a necessary condition for the attainment of moral state Z.'

The object of study is the moral development of the individual and its consequences for a society.

Each of these orientations has yielded some findings and interpretations of data supportive of its position. Yet much ambiguity remains, as reflected in the definitional attempts, in even the most current writing, to distinguish leisure from, say, recreation (Klausner, 1969). Moreover, there is a clearly recognizable perjorative element common to all of these orientations. That is, leisure is that which remains after work is completed. Though a number of variations may be found, most definitions share this element in essence. This situation is not unusual, for often inquiry into new areas of study employs concepts largely derivative from previously investigated areas of interest and also everyday language.

Within sociology, the theoretical importance placed upon work and work-related aspects for understanding the formation and functioning of societies has produced a large and informative literature. Indeed, the sociology of work has been refined into a variety of sociologies such as occupations, complex organizations, and industrial societies. The emergence and development of appropriate psychologies, social and otherwise, occurred simultaneously. The study of leisure and recreation, mass or individual, has attempted to develop within this larger theoretical stream. The consensus, as indicated above, is that the attempts to date are largely abortive. What few unambiguous findings may exist have failed to suggest any theoretically interesting or unique characteristics of this amorphously defined area of human activity (Neilsen, 1969).

Perhaps some of the difficulty lies in the implicit acceptance of leisure as a cafeteria concept residual, by definition, to work. Logic reminds us that the negative of a positive is "not-something." In an effort to rethink the theoretical issues raised by a study of leisure patterns, it may be useful to adopt a similar terminology for expository purposes. Thus, in the remaining portion of this paper, we will attempt to examine the theoretical negation of work. Instead of leisure, recreation, play, free time, or what have you, we will employ the concept of 'not-work.' The theoretical pair is thus comprised of 'work' and 'not-work.'

'WORK' AND 'NOT-WORK': A COMPARISON OF CONSTRUCTS

Meyersohn (1969: 55) noted that in the studies of leisure "little effort has been made to study *groups* [*emphasis* in original] as such" and "like much other social research has been based largely on random samples, in which the *connectedness of humans* [*emphasis* added] is carefully sampled out." These comments, along with others examined above, suggest one likely place to begin the examination of the theoretical pair is in terms of their respective social organizations.

The strategy we are employing is to begin to try to distinguish between the social organization of work and the social organization of not-work. We will leave the question of their interrelationships, if any, until later. Clearly, we cannot begin to explicate in detail all of the possible similarities and differences which may or may not exist between this pair of theoretical constructs. As such we will focus upon a limited set, largely contrasting the pair. This set includes:

(1) the elementary sociological unit upon which the social organizations rest;

(2) the social indices of the distribution of approval and deference among participants;

(3) the socioemotional basis upon which approval accrues to participants; and

(4) the sociologically defined minimal characteristics of a participant.

Before the content of this set is discussed, it is necessary to distinguish among an individual, a social person, and a social group.

Human individuals, like other animals, are sentient beings. As biological animals, they experience the arousal of emotions, hunger pangs, sexual urges, and so on. Taking these factors into account, for our purposes, an individual refers to the skin-bounded organism, a member of the species homo sapiens. Comparatively, a social person is that particular combination of social roles an individual develops over his lifetime. Thus, the composition of a social personage may vary among individuals and for a single individual between one phase of his development and another. Quite literally, the same individual may be a different person at one time or another.[1] Certainly, the development and expression of individualism as it occurs socially and psychologically is more than biological, but its emergence and dynamics are beyond this discussion. It is noteworthy, however, that the process of socialization is precisely the formation and transformation of social personages. Finally, a social group is comprised of individuals who define themselves as members and are defined by others as members (Merton, 1957). With these terms clarified, we are now prepared to consider the comparison between the social organization of work and not-work. Chart 1 provides a summary of the discussion to follow.

Work refers to behavior generally participated in by the social person, usually, although not exclusively, as an adult or subadult,[2] for which social approval is received. Social approval is symbolized by access to the market (class), social honors (status), and influence over the behavior of other social persons (power). Approval accrues for participation in the activities as a social person enacting the rights and obligations of appropriate social roles in particular situations. A society may be thought of as partially comprised of institutions in which work is a central characteristic—e.g., economic and political institutions. These institutions are partially comprised of complex organizations where much of work behavior occurs—e.g., factories, banks, city halls. Other societal institutions have a

CHART I
SOCIAL ORGANIZATION OF:

	Work	Not-Work
Unit	Social Person	Social Group
Indications of social approval	Access to market (class)	Sharing of goods (exchange of social favors)
	Social honor (status)	Gesture of appreciation (smiling, touching, etc.)
	Influence over the behavior of others (power)	Nonspecific leadership (communion)
Socioemotional basis	Enactment of social role	Consciousness of kind (solidarity)
Minimal social characteristic	Adults, subadults	Adults, subadults, juveniles, infants

work component, but include additional behavior not yet discussed. Such institutions are those of a religious and educational nature, where approval is also accrued for adequate or inadequate social role enactment.

The theoretical opposite of work is not leisure, but not-work. Not-work refers to behavior generally participated in by social groups. Such groups are usually comprised of adults, subadults, juveniles, and infants. Participants are individuals. Social approval is symbolized among the groups and participants by exchange of social favors (sharing of goods), gestures of appreciation (for example, smiling, touching, laughing), and communion (nonspecific leadership or direction). Approval accrues for participation as an individual and a group member through activities which build interindividual identification and generate intergroup solidarity creating a consciousness of kind among all participants. Societies have some institutions in which not-work is characteristic—e.g., leisure and familial. In others, as those of a religious nature, not-work and work may occur together, but for different participants.

To increase the understanding of our argument, recall that our comparison is between two constructs of social organization. Note that the differences between the basic social structural units of social person and social group are pivotal to our concerns. It is the thrust of this argument that continued inattention to this fundamental structural difference has produced much of the ambiguity in the studies of leisure to date. We believe that research oriented to this difference can provide new insights into the social behavior of man and the manner in which his societies are integrated. Before considering this topic, let us examine a recent study which suggests the theoretical power of the distinction under consideration.

LEISURE STUDIES REVISITED

William Burch (1969), in a recent article, appears to express some of the same concerns as Meyersohn. Burch sought to evaluate the comparative explanatory power of several competing hypotheses with reference to the style of camping in which respondents were engaged. First, he examined the compensatory explanation which suggested that camping style should reflect sharp differences from the respondent's regular routine. Secondly, the familiarity hypothesis was examined. This explanation suggests the respondent's camping style should reflect his familiar pattern of living. Burch concluded that neither hypothesis was supported sufficiently to warrant discarding other explanations. In fact, Burch observed the empirical tendency for the data to converge in a manner suggestive of the importance of social interactional contexts. This led him to examine a third hypothesis which he designated the "personal community" explanation. Briefly, once he began to consider the family of procreation and the family of orientation as the unit of analysis qua social groups, his understanding of antecedent conditions influencing camping style increased. Unfortunately, his data did not permit an exhaustive test of the comparative explanatory power of the propositions. It is noteworthy, however, that in his analysis Burch moved from assessing camping styles as related to attributes of social persons to occupational milieux and then to social groups. Burch concluded that the analysis of leisure patterns, using the social group as a unit of analysis, provides a promising line of inquiry.

There is no doubt that some portion of the variance in studies of leisure behavior will always be accounted for through an emphasis on social personages. What the work of Burch suggests is that much more of the variance is explainable if we do not stop there.

Perhaps one of the most intriguing statements in Burch's article is found in a footnote (1969: 146), where he considers the possibility that leisure values (left undefined by him) may persist analogously, over generations, to religious values held within a particular family. He mentions that many of his respondents expressed attitudes about nature and camping best described as religious in character. The argument being developed in this paper would clearly suggest such sentiments should have been found. Moreover, such expressions could only have been engendered in situations where the respondent was caught up as an individual in a social group sharing what may be termed "initimate sociability."

Before examining the question of how the social organization of work and not-work may be integrated, it is interesting to notice that this argument enables us to place the previously mentioned theoretical perspectives common to much contemporary leisure research within a larger framework. One explanation for the present state of the sociology of leisure, as depicted by Meyersohn, may lie in the utilization of the least appropriate unit of observation—that is, the social person. In a recent study conducted by the author of this article, data were obtained which further suggest the utility of the distinction we have been discussing.

The study is part of a series of investigations of the sociological aspects of the sociocultural behavior of going to parks and zoos. This study attempts to identify how such behavior is or is not related to other aspects of the social institutions in a society. The data consist of about 1,000 interviews obtained from an area probability sample of adults, eighteen years and older, residing at the time of the study in the continental United States. These data are in the preliminary stages of analysis and for our purposes here, we will report on only some data from adult males. There are 444 males in the sample.

Assuming that going to a local park is an operationalization of not-work, let us consider what we can learn about this behavior by knowing what the occupation (an aspect of a social person) of the respondent might be. For the sake of simplicity a summary measure is used—blue-collar/white-collar. This is cross-tabulated with whether the respondent had or had not gone to a local park, used as a measure of participation, within the preceding two years. Table 1 shows the results.

As can be seen, there is no significant difference between the occupational categories. Knowing whether the respondent has a blue- or white-collar occupation tells us little about his participation in park-going. One reason may be that we are

TABLE 1
MALE PARTICIPATION IN GOING TO A LOCAL PARK,
BY OCCUPATION

Occupation	In Local Park	Not in Local Park	n
Blue-collar	164	61	225
White-collar	156	63	219
Total	320	124	444

$$X^2 = .0801 \quad 1 \text{ df} \quad \text{n.s.}$$

measuring the incorrect theoretical unit appropriate for the phenomenon under study.

Earlier we argued that work and not-work were organized around differing sociological units. Recall Meyersohn's comments about our research often filtering out the "connectedness" among humans. In Table 2, we examine, among those 320 males who had gone to a local park, whether they went alone or with others. In Table 3, we examine their behavior when traveling to place of employment. The comparison shows that clearly, going to a local park is something done as a member of a social grouping.

These data are suggestive that going to work and going to a local park are structurally quite different. This paper argues that such a difference is theoretically fundamental and that our inquiries will be strengthened if we begin to systematically incorporate such concerns into our investigations.

In an attempt to ascertain some comparative assessment of other not-work settings, the respondents were asked if they participated in other kinds of activities during the year preceding the study and, if so, whether they participated alone or with others. Thus, in Table 4, the number of respondents varies among the activities, since all did not participate to the same extent during the specified time interval. It is clear, though, that for those who participated, over seventy percent did so with others in all activities. In short, it is unlikely that going to a local park is an empirically unique example of a not-work setting. It shares a common social structural characteristic with several other settings.

TABLE 2
MALE PARTICIPATION IN GOING TO A LOCAL PARK

Activity	Alone	With Others	n
Going to park	60	260	320

$x^2 = 125.00$	1 df	significant beyond .01

TABLE 3
MALE PARTICIPATION IN EMPLOYMENT

Activity	Alone	With Others	n
Going to work	246	74	320

$x^2 = 92.44$	1 df	significant beyond .01

THE INTEGRATION OF SOCIAL SYSTEMS

One of the important contributions that any particular area of inquiry can make to a larger body of knowledge is to enable research questions to be formulated which increase the understanding of the general theoretical problems of the discipline. In view of the previous comments in this paper, it seems appropriate to discuss how the proposed distinction between the social organization of work and not-work might contribute to general sociological questions.

One of the most vexatious problems for sociology has been how a social order is held together. Functionalism has, to date, provided the most articulate answers to the query. Yet the problematics of functionalism suggest the implicit weaknesses of such arguments wherever they appear in science. Integration of any social system refers to the ways in which the parts of that system are interrelated in such a manner as to produce a theoretically unique and identifiable structure. Hopefully, such structures, in time, have empirical referents.

The theoretical position developed in this paper suggests that the social behavior of homo sapiens can be seen as comprised of work and not-work. It has been suggested that each phase is characteristically ordered and integrated. Thus, work is integrated among social personages and not-work among social

TABLE 4
DEGREE OF SOCIAL PARTICIPATION BY MALES IN A
VARIETY OF NOT-WORK ACTIVITIES

Activity	Participated: Percentages:				
Going to:	With Others	Alone	Both	No Response	n
Movies	84.0	6.2	6.3	3.5	289
Local park	78.5	9.7	8.3	3.5	281
Sporting event	75.0	9.8	12.0	3.2	267
Visiting friends	74.4	9.7	13.5	2.4	423
Church	72.3	15.8	10.1	1.8	318
Nightclub, bar, etc.	77.4	7.4	13.2	2.0	229

groups. The basic unit for each phase is different. Moreover, there exists some reason to believe that this twofold division, in terms of social organization, may not be unique in all its aspects to human societies alone.

The distinction between social persons and social groups, both of which are "inhabited" by individual homo sapiens, may reflect the operation of two broad principles of social organization often observed among other species. Glen McBride (1964) has noted that homo sapiens as a species tends to diverge from a characteristic pattern of social organization found among most others. That pattern is one in which the members of the group remain more or less constant but in which the group's social structure varies in carrying out necessary functions. An example is the change in the characteristic social relationships among baboon troop members when the reproductive phase is active. Homo sapiens, unlike many other species, appears to be group-forming. That is, individual members pass from one group to another in a social structure where groups remain constant for specific functions. The important aspect of McBride's insight lies in his emphasis on the social group and its relation to the individual member of a species. As noted above, we differ somewhat from McBride's position, in that within societies of homo sapiens, both of these principles of social organization appear to operate. Indeed, it is this duality which may be an important analytical distinction among the various social species.

Finally, it is important to note that the common element through which work and not-work are integrated, such that we may speak of social solidarity sufficiently succinctly to recognize a human society, is the individual qua individual. Having said this, what are the implications for research on human leisure patterns?

We can now begin to see how systematic studies of not-work can also make new and theoretically relevant contributions to sociology per se. For example, mechanisms of intergroup interaction can be investigated, once it is recognized that some social institutions develop only where the fundamental organizing social unit is a social group. The general theoretical problem of how societies are held together is worthy of additional thought, bearing the distinction between work and not-work in mind. Finally, many opportunities for theoretically relevant interchanges between the biology of homo sapiens and the sociology of the species can be developed. One example is the manner in which man's biologically grounded sociability is convergent with his culturally grounded sociability.

CONCLUSION

In this paper, we have discussed some of the difficulties that research in the sociology of leisure has shared, in an attempt to define its problems in a manner most conducive to the broader theoretical concerns of how societies are organized and integrated. It has been suggested that inattention to a basic social organizational difference between work and not-work may help to account for some of the difficulties, as well as providing a point of theoretical departure from which future studies may start. Finally, we have suggested ways in which recognition of this difference in social organization may lead to an increased understanding of the more general problematics of societies and social systems common among several social species.

NOTES

1. The usage of social person as here employed is reminiscent of Robert Merton's status set and status sequence. However, the present usage attempts to highlight the

individual's idiosyncratic contribution to a status set, reflecting the intensities of emotional arousal as an important aspect for all participants. It is this kind of thing which is seen in the historical distinctions between "strong" and "weak" presidents of various organizations (see Merton, 1957).

2. The use of terms adult, subadult, juvenile, and so on, are employed to denote social age classes. They are used analogously to their use in ethology and some studies in wildlife management. Basically, they refer to social age categories known to individuals in a society. In short, expectations regarding social interaction are considerably developed if ego and alter know only the social age class of each other. An approximate distribution of chronological age with social age can be suggested: infant (birth to 6 years); juvenile (7-17 years); subadult (18-24 years); adult (25-49 years); and, mature adult (50 years and older).

REFERENCES

Bishop, Doyle and Masaru Ikeda
    1970 "Status and role factors in the leisure behavior of different occupations." Sociology and Social Research 43 (January): 190-208.
Burch, William R., Jr.
    1969 "The social circles of leisure: competing explanations." J. of Leisure Research 1 (Spring): 125-147.
DeGrazia, Sebastian
    1962 Of Time, Work and Leisure. New York: Twentieth Century Fund.
Havighurst, Robert J.
    1957 "The leisure activities of the middle-aged." Amer. J. of Sociology 62 (September): 152-162.
Klausner, Samuel Z.
    1969 "Recreation as social action." In a Program for Outdoor Recreation in Research. Washington, D.C.: National Academy of Sciences.
McBride, Glen
    1964 A General Theory of Social Organization and Behavior. St. Lucia, Australia: Univ. of Queensland Press.
Merton, Robert
    1957 Social Theory and Social Structure. Glencoe, Ill.: Free Press.
Meyersohn, Rolf
    1969 "The sociology of leisure in the United States: introduction and bibliography, 1945-1965." J. of Leisure Research 1 (Winter): 53-68.
Neilsen, Joyce
    1969 "Towards a sociological theory of forest recreation." M.A. thesis. University of Washington.
Weiss, Paul
    1969 Sport: A Philosophic Inquiry. Carbondale: Southern Illinois Univ. Press.

A FUNCTION OF UNCERTAINTY
AND STAKES IN RECREATION

JO M. SENTERS

Washington State Department of Social and Health Services

Recreation **as a field** of behavior and values has been relatively unexplored by social scientists. As late as 1965, it was suggested in a major sociological journal that recreation does indeed reflect social processes traditionally studied by sociologists and affords opportunities to study theories of the middle range (Burch, 1965).

In this paper, two concepts, *uncertainty* and *stakes,* are investigated as they relate to a theoretical orientation toward recreation. After establishing the conceptual boundaries of the field of interest—recreation—the potential importance of the two concepts will be examined.

Recreation and leisure are not considered to be synonymous. Leisure implies a temporal dimension—that time free from the more formal and obligatory demands of work (Lundberg et al., 1934: 2; Anderson, 1961: 33). Recreation, however, refers to a behavioral dimension—engaging in mental or physical activity for its own sake, where moderately uncertain outcome and stakes add value to the activity. "Engaging in an activity for its own sake" refers to the value intrinsic in an activity as perceived

AUTHOR'S NOTE: *This paper has been developed out of research undertaken for the author's Master's thesis, "Conditions Associated With Risktaking: A Field Study," University of Washington, Seattle, 1970.*

by the performer. The history of the performer's assignment of value to this activity is not of immediate interest and is assumed to have been learned through typical processes of socialization (e.g., sanctions operating within a peer group to ensure conformity).

"Moderately uncertain outcome" means that the probability of an event occurring is about 0.5. This condition is realized when winning or losing in an activity is nearly equal, such as the case where opponents are similar in ability or subject to the same chance conditions. This meaning of uncertainty is dependent on the performer's assessment; uncertainty is assumed to be a cognitive state reflecting current communication from the environment, past experiences, and perception. The complexities of subjective versus psychological probability will not be confronted here (see Cohen and Christensen, 1970: 25-57).

"Stakes" refer to the consequences of an event occurring. While simply winning or losing may be the sole outcome (consequence) of a game, there may be others, such as payment on a bet.

Some social scientists have suggested that moderate uncertainty and stakes have an influence on the value of recreational or similar activities. Berlyne (1960) examined research on skill tasks and concluded that individuals set goals located near the upper limits of their abilities—at a point where success carries a probability of near 0.5. White (1959) suggests animals, including man, enjoy challenge and seek activities of moderate uncertainty. Schwartz (1967: 9-10), in his examination of the norm of reciprocity and gift-giving, concluded that moderate uncertainty plays an essential role in this behavior: "Without suspense, the entire tone of the gift exchange is altered—and with it, the relationship, which is correspondingly deprived of its mystery and suprise." Caillois (1961: 7) specified uncertainty as an essential part of his definition of play: "An outcome known in advance . . . is incompatible with the nature of play." Utilizing data obtained from a mountain-climbing expedition, Emerson (1966) presented a theory which suggests that sustained group goal-striving is a function of uncertainty about goal outcome.

It is submitted here that moderate uncertainty and stakes both serve to increase the value of a recreational activity and, further, that a "maturation phenomenon" occurs such that in the course of engaging in an activity persons alter their behavior to ensure that the conditions of play (uncertainty) and the outcome (stakes) continue to add value. Such an approach to recreation permits the presence of excitement, tension, and extreme effort, unlike the premise that recreation serves primarily as tension relaxation and the absence of anxiety (Nye, 1958; Crespi, 1956).

THE RESEARCH SETTING

The focus of the present study is on the risk-taking behavior of a small group of working-class males as they engaged in recreation. This tavern-based recreation is located in a major population center in the Pacific Northwest.

The research was designed as a longitudinal case study. Six men were observed over a period of one-and-one-half years as they played the game of table shuffleboard. Shuffleboard is a competitive game, the outcome of which depends primarily on the skill of the players, although random factors influence the outcome to some degree. Players oppose one another singly, in pairs, or in small groups.

Data collecting occurred as the group evolved through processes of group formation, consensus over behavior and goals, and termination. Data collection was through participant observation with supplementation by reliable records of performance, consisting of scores written down at the time of play by a scorer with frequent checking by other group members and the performer himself.

Observation in the tavern setting was provided through the cooperation of a habitué, a neighbor of the author. This person occupied an important leadership position in the group from its inception, and the author, with a similar working-class background, was accepted as one of a small group of habitual observers to shuffleboard games. The author's research role was not revealed to the participants. No research problems were perceived as arising from emotional involvement with the subjects (compare Glass and Frankiel, 1968), perhaps because the researcher filled a legitimate role in the setting: one of several passive female observers of a game of skill actively played by working-class men. None of the persons in the setting was single or competing for sexual favors.

FINDINGS

Information gained through participant observation will be discussed first, and then that obtained through analysis of performance records will be presented.

CHANGING THE OUTCOME TO INCREASE THE VALUE

Players were observed to increase the value of the shuffleboard game by increasing the stakes. While learning the game, the six players appeared to play for the rewards of play itself. They would practice aspects of the game alone or engage in competitive games with one or more others. This stage occurred as the men began to frequent the tavern regularly. In this first stage, the players were presumably testing and improving their skills. When one player suggested that they were skilled enough to compete as a team against other similar tavern-based teams within a shuffleboard league, the players readily agreed. Membership was stable in the team under study (hereafter referred to as "the team") and its opponent teams during the period of observation.

The second stage of shuffleboard playing was more formalized. The players were seen to engage very infrequently in the game for its own sake. At this point, the six played only under one of two conditions: (a) as a team competing against other teams in a structured league setting, following standardized rules of play; or (b) in smaller groups when bets were placed on outcomes.

The author concluded that the value of this well-practiced game had decreased for the participants in a manner analogous to psychological satiation, and that competitive team play and betting, each in its own way, increased the value of the game by increasing the stakes. The six players simply would not play shuffleboard unless one of these two conditions was met (League rules restricted players from engaging simultaneously in team play and betting).

Not only was there an overall change in the value attached to shuffleboard as the players became more skillful, but in any particular evening, a regular series of events occurred to temporarily increase the value of shuffleboard. During a typical evening, the initiator of a first bet would suggest playing "for beer." The next bet would be for a dollar or two. Subsequent bets would be for five or ten dollars. The following incident illustrates this process:

After the conclusion of league play one evening and after several five-dollar bets had been played, a relatively inexperienced player from an opponent team ("Jim") was observed to approach a member of the team under study ("Roy") Jim and Roy were thought to be of similar ability by other players and were well liked. Jim offered to play Roy for beer, but not for money. He offered several times but was refused each time in rather scornful tones. When Jim protested that he played shuffleboard for fun and not for money, Roy proclaimed: "You're in the wrong crowd then. You shouldn't be here. I either play for money or not at all." While playing for beer was acceptable to the experienced players when betting was initiated, stakes were expected to increase, at least gradually. The maximum bet considered reasonable in this group was in the ten- to twenty-dollar range. Playing shuffleboard without the added value of either betting or team (league) competition was described as "no fun."

CHANGING THE CONDITIONS TO INCREASE UNCERTAINTY

Performance records suggest that when the six men played as a team, they adjusted their performances so as to increase the uncertainty of outcomes. These records were available for analysis only during the second league season (year). The six members of the team competed individually against opponent team members, but scoring was based on pair-performance. These pairs met throughout the season in a "round robin" schedule of both opponents and location of play. Thus, records were measures of ability rather than of luck in drawing opponents or favored locations. The "subgames" engaged in by the pairs allowed for maximum sharing of responsibility by the six players in the ultimate win or loss of a game. The final outcome of a game utilized the scores of the eighteen subgames in a combination addition/bonus-point scheme.

The author was informed that the team had performed as a superior unit in league play the past season, and it was observed to always win in its second season. This team went on to win both league and state championships during the second season. On the basis of the team's high ratio of wins to losses, it was thought that analysis of the eighteen subgames per game might reveal relatively large margins of points over opponents. In Table 1, it can be seen that the magnitude of the means of differences over the eight games is not large. (Positive values were assigned to the means in the team's favor.)

Statistically, all teams were similar in abilities, as shown in Table 2. There is surprising variation reflected in the within/between variance ratios of 25.87 (P. = < .001), which indicates fluctuation in individual player performances as the subgames were played out.

It is suggested that feelings of superiority or confidence and the structure of shared responsibility may have served to increase the variance within the scoring distributions. Through close monitoring of the team's progress during a session, supplemented by discussion (environmental feedback), a particular player would not play to win. He could afford to perform poorly now and better later. Frequently observed was

TABLE 1

SUMMARY STATISTICS ON SUBGAME SCORING
DIFFERENCES BETWEEN THE STUDY TEAM AND ITS
OPPONENT TEAMS, FOR EIGHT GAMES

Statistic	Game							
	1	2	3	4	5	6	7	8
Sums	-10	+59	+63	+6	+37	+35	+12	-2
Means	-.55	3.27	3.5	.33	2.05	1.94	.66	.11
n	18	18	18	18	18	18	18	18
Standard deviation	8.88	7.94	6.27	8.22	8.16	9.11	5.27	8.44

TABLE 2

ANALYSIS OF VARIANCE ON THE MEANS OF SCORE
DIFFERENCES BETWEEN TEAM UNDER STUDY AND ITS
OPPONENT TEAMS, FOR EIGHT GAMES

Variance	Sums of Squares	Degrees of Freedom	Estimate of Variance	F Ratio
Total	9,167.24	143	—	—
Between	18.21	7	2.60	B/W = .003
Within	9,149	136	67.27	W/B = 25.87
				P. = $<$.001

NOTE: Differences of subgame scores.

the norm of "carrying a player," which means that if one member of a pair were playing poorly, the other member would volunteer or be asked to offset any losses by trying harder. There was great consensus on the legitimacy of this norm.

Opponent teams assessed as easy to beat did not warrant increased points—even though increased points favorably influenced the league standing of the team under study. Indeed, the opposite case was observed to occur. One opponent team was perceived as so poor that the team under study deliberately let it obtain a large lead and then played very hard to win the session by a *small* margin. While this strategy was not completely verbalized, there were frequent references to careless playing as "okay . . . because there's still time to beat these guys." Such nonmaximization, utilizing environmental feedback, is seen to increase the uncertainty of the final outcome (win or loss of the game) by equalizing performances of the two teams in a manner similar to the handicap given in other sports (for example, golf). Complementing this nonmaximization of performance was the team's approach to its opponents. Prior to a game, the opponent team was discussed with the bravado, nervousness, and excitement associated with competitive skill games where the outcome is uncertain.

DISCUSSION AND CONCLUSION

It is concluded from this study that the players studied engaged in shuffleboard for the pleasure of the game itself until they became relatively well skilled. Then, essentially, they rejected the previous sole stakes (win or loss) by demanding that this group activity be conducted only when stakes were increased through a competitive league structure or through betting.

The players continually adjusted their performances to ensure an ongoing level of uncertainty in the final outcomes of the league games. They developed patterns of interaction (the norm of carrying a player) and communication (jargon) relating to examination of their progress according to the score sheets.

These findings suggest that man requires a certain level of uncertainty with which to test his own talents and responses, and that changing the consequences or outcome of behavior is interdependent with uncertainty. If this is valid, then where men have a choice of activities, as in recreation, they will seek opportunities for consequent challenge. The concept of uncertainty is especially important to the sociological study of change. If persons individually or in groups prefer certain levels of uncertainty, they will be motivated to maintain it where present, and to seek it where it is absent through the examination of alternatives. An example of the latter might be found in the sociological study of the small group, where the deviant is rejected. Emerson (1968) evaluated previous interpretations based on balance theory, and concluded that repetition, rather than deviant opinions, led to the rejection of nonconforming members of such groups. The decreasing value of repetitious remarks was also illustrated in a member of the shuffleboard team under study. High frequency of remarks containing no new information contributed to the player's unpopularity. A definite negative emotional response was generated in his listeners. The players were observed to make efforts to change the repetitive speaker by forming coalitions and engaging in punishing communication and avoidance behavior.

Researchers may well include gambling as a type of recreation, rather than as deviant behavior. Lower-class individuals in America, for example, have been portrayed in the literature as seeking escape from lives deprived of meaningful activities; that is, gambling provides a deviant escape from hours of work and leisure filled with boredom and the routine of industrial life (Bloch, 1951; Zola, 1963). It is suggested that gambling be viewed as the seeking and maintaining of uncertain conditions where opportunities in the setting consist mainly of betting on games of chance or skill.

If a player perceives an outcome to be influenced by his own actions, he may persist longer than if he realizes that the outcome is based only on random factors. Field studies of gambling, where outcome is based almost solely on chance, show this remarkably persistent behavior is associated with strategies which are thought by the players to affect the outcomes (Scott, 1968; Zola, 1963). Players of these chance games (on-track and off-track betting of horses) did not perceive the outcome as based only on chance. It is interesting in this regard that in studies of response rate (which can be interpreted as one indicator of motivation to perform), one hundred percent reinforcement typically leads to satiation and extinction. Where subjects perceived a task as within their control, however, one hundred percent reinforcement led to less rapid extinction than did fifty percent reinforcement (James and Rotter, 1958).

Stakes as a concept separate from uncertainty are less general than the latter and refer more directly to value attached to an activity's outcome based on the particular history of the performer or the performing group. While both stakes and uncertainty are hypothesized to add value to an activity, stakes may be more dependent on variables such as socioeconomic status and goals. While the shuffleboard players placed bets on their games, businessmen, for example, might add very different stakes to their recreational activities.

Admittedly, there are conceptual difficulties for the sociologist in studying the variables of uncertainty and stakes. Psychologists have long been concerned with the complexities of objective, subjective, and psychological probability, the issues of achievement motivation, and the hypothesized variation in preferred uncertainty levels across individuals and over time. Yet the concepts of stakes and uncertainty appear as amenable to study as such accepted concepts as "dissonance" and "self-image," although the latter two may be subject to similar variation. It is suggested that uncertainty, at a moderate level, is of particular importance to the study of recreation wherein individuals exhibit choice behavior.

Recreation is frequently described as providing the settings in which extraordinary demands are made on the individual (Burch, 1965; Brewster, 1970). Perhaps an essential attribute of "extraordinary" is riskiness or uncertainty. Further research on moderate uncertainty and stakes in recreation patterns, particularly on a longitudinal basis, seems warranted.

REFERENCES

Anderson, Nels
    1961 Work and Leisure. Glencoe, Ill.: Free Press.
Berlyne, Donald
    1960 Conflict, Arousal and Curiosity. New York: McGraw-Hill.
Bloch, Herbert
    1951 "Sociology of gambling." Amer. J. of Sociology 57 (November): 215-222.

Brewster, David
  1970 "Jews write novels; Irishmen run cities; WASPS camp."
        Seattle Magazine 7 (June): 25-31.
Burch, William
  1965 "The play world of camping: research into the social
        meaning of outdoor recreation." Amer. J. of Sociology 70
        (March): 604-612.
Caillois, Roger
  1961 Man, Play and Games. Glencoe, Ill.: Free Press.
Cohen, John and Ian Christensen
  1970 Information and Choice. Edinburgh: Oliver & Boyd.
Crespi, Irving
  1956 "The social significance of card playing as a leisure time
        activity." Amer. Soc. Rev. 21 (December): 717-721.
Emerson, Richard
  1966 "Mount Everest: a case study of communication feedback
        and sustained group goal-striving." Sociometry 29 (Sep-
        tember): 213-227.
  1968 "Role theory and diminishing utility in group problem-
        solving." Pacific Soc. Rev. 11 (Fall): 110-115.
Glass, John and Harry Frankiel
  1968 "The influence of subjects on the researcher: a problem in
        observing social interaction." Pacific Soc. Rev. 11 (Fall):
        75-80.
James, William and J. B. Rotter
  1958 "Partial and 100% reinforcement under chance and skill
        conditions." J. of Experimental Psychology 55 (May):
        397-403.
Lundberg, George, Mirra Komarovsky, and Mary McInerny
  1934 Leisure: A Suburban Study. New York: Columbia Univ.
        Press.
Nye, F. Ivan
  1958 "Employment status and recreational behavior of mothers."
        Pacific Soc. Rev. 1 (Fall): 69-72.
Schwartz, Barry
  1967 "The social psychology of the gift." Amer. J. of Sociology
        73 (July): 1-11.
Scott, Marvin
  1968 The Racing Game. Chicago: Aldine.
White, Robert
  1959 "Motivation reconsidered: the concept of competence."
        Psych. Rev. 66 (September): 297-330.
Zola, Kevin
  1963 "Observations on gambling in a lower class setting." Social
        Problems 10 (Spring): 353-361.

THE ENVIRONMENTAL MOVEMENT

From Recreation to Politics

RONALD G. FAICH
RICHARD P. GALE
University of Oregon

Seen from the perspective of leisure-time activity, the rapidly emerging environmental movement has several important implications for future research in the sociology of leisure. First, a number of people are expending substantial amounts of their nonwork time on behalf of the environment. Second, because much involvement is channeled through voluntary organizations, participation in the environmental movement must be considered within the context of the structure of voluntary organizations and their contribution to ongoing social movements. Third, the protection of areas for outdoor recreation is a major focus of the environmental movement.[1] The increasing public concern with environmental issues and the role that leisure-time organizations play in the movement suggest that social scientists interested in the sociology of leisure should direct some attention to the changing role of such organizations. Of particular interest in this regard would be the changing organizational goals of outdoor recreation groups and the political implications of these changes. The intent of this paper is to assess the limited previous research and theoretical development in this area, to report the preliminary results of a membership survey of a large outdoor recreation organization which is rapidly changing, and to suggest future needs in research and theory.

OUTDOOR RECREATION AND THE ENVIRONMENTAL
MOVEMENT

Past research on outdoor-oriented leisure has focused mainly on the characteristics of recreationists (Burch, 1969), the specific activities engaged in (King, 1966), the frequency of outdoor recreation, and some of the motivations and meanings attached to it (Burch, 1965).

When previous investigators have examined the organizational memberships of outdoor recreationists, it has usually been limited to determining the proportion of recreationists who belong to some type of outdoor recreation group. Several studies report that about a third of the recreationists studied claim membership in some outdoor recreation or conservation group (Hendee et al., 1968; ORRRC, 1962; LaPage, 1967). Of secondary interest has been the diversity of organizations cited whenever recreationists are asked to list their recreation and conservation organization memberships. The 408 wilderness users in the Hendee et al. (1968) study belonged to 218 different groups, and many individuals cross-listed the same organization as both an outdoor recreation and a conservation organization. Although the Hendee group did not distinguish between outdoor recreation and conservation groups in their analysis, they did suggest a "stepping-stone" process whereby individuals initially joined local activity-oriented outdoor recreation groups, and later expanded their involvement in the conservation—now environmental—movement by joining large national organizations (Hendee et al., 1968: 21).

Most relevant to this paper is the body of research which places the study of outdoor recreation organizations in the context of the analysis of voluntary organizations. Variations of the instrumental-expressive distinction have been used to assess both the goals and the activities of the organization and the expectations and participation of the members of such organizations.[2] For example, Jacoby and Babchuk (1963: 468) describe a hiking club in which member participation was almost exclusively expressive, and members "apologized for the uselessness of their hiking club activities." Yet when the charter of the club and minutes of its meetings were examined, there was some evidence of instrumental action by the organization, although it was still considered primarily an expressive group by the investigators. In a later article, perhaps thinking of the same organization, Babchuk states, "But a hiking club by virtue of sending a resolution to a congressional representative on a conservation bill hardly qualifies by that token as an instrumental association" (Babchuk and Edwards, 1965: 155). It would be our contention that the environmental movement has probably changed the orientation of that hiking club, and that if Jacoby and Babchuk were to study the same club in 1971, they would find increased instrumental involvement, including, besides sending a resolution to a congressional representative, possible affiliation with a statewide environmental council, the solicitation of statements from congressional candidates on environmental issues, surveillance of a governmental agency with environmental responsibilities, and even possibly the filing of an injunction to protect a favorite hiking area.

In an attempt to categorize those outdoor recreation organizations which reflect varying degrees of instrumental involvement with environmental issues, Hendee et al. (1969) have applied the instrumental-expressive distinction to both organizations and their individual members.[3] The term "expressive conservationist" is used to describe members and groups whose instrumental concerns are confined to actions directly related to the primary recreation goals of the organization. Thus, for example, a group of kyackers may become involved in a controversy over a dam proposed along one of their favorite rivers, but resist involvement in an effort to block construction of a highway. "Instrumental conservationists," on the other hand, may also participate in outdoor recreation but they concentrate primarily on the "protection of areas and environments that members themselves may not have visited" (Hendee et al., 1969: 213). Instrumental conservation organizations are generally involved in a wide variety of environmental issues, and often considerable authority is delegated to executive committees to formulate positions on these issues and to represent the organization publicly.

The instrumental-expressive distinction as applied to these groups includes four related variables. Most obvious is the way in which the membership views the organization, reflected in the reasons why persons initially join the organization and the factors which sustain their active support. Expressive organizations would attract members primarily seeking outdoor recreation activities and companionship, while more instrumental organizations would draw members sympathetic with the organization's external action program. The second variable is the amount of member participation in organizational activities, and in the formal governance of the organization. In expressive conservation organizations, one would expect to find a high level of participation, and a broadly diffused administrative structure, while more instrumental groups would reflect a low level of direct participation and a highly concentrated leadership network. The emphasis on outdoor recreation in organizational programs is the third variable. More expressive organizations would maintain an extensive outing program, and the membership would be recruited from individuals who are active outdoor recreationists. In instrumentally oriented groups, on the other hand, such outing programs would concentrate on visits to disputed areas, and members may not be outdoor recreation enthusiasts, in spite of their strong support of recreation-related environmental issues. Finally, the fourth variable concerns the total involvement of the members in various instrumental and expressive organizations related to outdoor recreation and the environment. We would not expect members of one expressive organization to belong to many other similar groups because of the high level of participation within these recreation-oriented clubs. On the other hand, members of a more instrumental organization, lending their support to the group's position on issues, and not necessarily participating directly in the operation of the group, may well extend their commitment to a variety of instrumental organizations concerned with environmental protection.

The distinction between instrumental and expressive conservation, and the four variables which further elaborate this distinction, form the basis for the analysis which follows. We suggest that some of the leisure-based outdoor recreation organizations which were initially dedicated to expressive, membership-oriented goals, will increasingly become instrumentally involved in the environmental movement. Where organizations undergo this transformation, we would expect to find similar changes in the expectations of the membership, the level of participation in the organization, and in the involvement of the members in outdoor recreation as a leisure-time activity. Ideally, a test of this general hypothesis would rely on a diachronic analysis of an expressive outdoor recreation organization. Unfortunately, this type of systematic data is not available, in part because of the very rapid growth of the environmental movement in the past two years. Instead, we draw on data from a sample survey of the membership of a large national organization which has, in the past several years, become involved in a variety of environmental issues, even though the organization was for many years very similar to the "expressive conservation" model, and still maintains an extensive outing program. To obtain some indication of change in membership, we will compare members in terms of the amount of time they have been members of the organization. Although this approach to an analysis of change involves some readily challengeable assumptions, we believe the data are suitable for a preliminary examination of the distinctions discussed previously.

THE PUGET SOUND GROUP OF THE SIERRA CLUB

The data to be reported in this paper were drawn from an internal survey conducted by a regional section of a large national outdoor recreation and environmental organization. The Sierra Club began before the turn of the century, as an expressive conservationist organization with a membership concentrated in California, particularly within the San Franciso Bay Area (Jones, 1965). The club had a long history of involvement in issues which were of direct concern to the wilderness recreation enthusiasts who constituted most of the membership. The extensive outing program reinforced member commitment to basic preservationist goals. About 1955, the club began to acquire a national membership, and to extend its instrumental activity into issues not necessarily related to wilderness recreation. In 1971, the club had over 100,000 members throughout the United States and had been "declared" an (excessively) instrumental conservationist organization by the Internal Revenue Service, which revoked the tax-deductible status of the club.

There are two component units in the club—the chapter and the group. Initially, Sierra Club members in California communities joined together to form local chapters of the club. When the club began to acquire a membership outside the state of California, new chapters were formed, usually on a regional basis. As chapters grew, members who were concentrated in large population centers within a region sought to form locally based units. Then the group became the local unit and regional chapters are now frequently composed of a number of widely dispersed local groups.

As of 1971, the Pacific Northwest Chapter of the Sierra Club had nearly 2,500 members in the state of Oregon and the western part of Washington. Of the six local groups within the chapter, the largest is the Puget Sound Group, with nearly 700 members living in the Seattle-Tacoma metropolitan area. Though only one of numerous environmental organizations in the area, the Puget Sound Group is one of the best known groups of this type because of its extensive outing program and frequent pronouncements on environmental issues. Though no group or chapter can be said to be "typical" of the Sierra Club, it is possible, however, that members of the Puget Sound Group may be somewhat more instrumentally oriented than their fellow members in other areas. In the Los Angeles area, for example, the club is a major outing organization but less well known for its political activities. The involvement of the Puget Sound Group is further reinforced by the fact that the club's Northwest Conservation Representative is headquartered in Seattle. Rather than viewing our respondents as representative either of members of the entire Sierra Club or of other outdoor recreation organizations, in general, they should be seen as reflecting a perspective which, we would argue, will increasingly pervade those individuals who seek to implement their hopes for a better environment through membership in an instrumental voluntary organization.

Although the response rate to the mail questionnaire was far from optimal (45%), and the survey was designed to obtain data on membership interests in environmental issues and club activities, the data are of sufficient quality to permit an exploration of questions emerging from previous research. After briefly examining the demographic characteristics of the membership, we will discuss data which bear on each of the four variables outlined above.

THE RESPONDENTS

As found in previous studies of the Sierra Club (Hendee et al., 1968) and other outing-conservation groups (Devall, 1970a, 1970b), the members of the Puget Sound Group are noteworthy for their high levels of educational attainment and occupational status. Professional positions are held by fully 73.8% of our respondents, an additional 9.8% are administrators and 9.2% students; only 2.8% are clerical workers and another 2.8% are unemployed. A mere 3% of the members have never attended college, while 25% have doctorates, 45.5% have master's degrees, and 17.4% the baccalaureate. Though data on income levels were not obtained, the education and occupation distributions reveal rather clearly that members of the Puget Sound Group come predominantly from the upper-middle and upper socioeconomic strata.

Two-thirds of the respondents are male, and a similar proportion of the sample is married. Nearly half, 48.3%, are childless, and 46% have three or fewer children, mostly under age 18. One-half of our respondents are 30-44, with the modal group, 25% being 30-34. The members are rather evenly split between those who do and those who do not claim any church affiliation, with 38% citing membership in a Protestant denomination. And, finally, 42% of the respondents are independents, politically, one-third are Democrats and 24% identify themselves as Republicans. In summary, the profile of a typical Puget Sound Group member which emerges is that of a highly educated, married male in his early thirties, having no children or a small young family, in a high-status occupational position, and who is likely to be independent on both politcal and religious matters.

REASONS FOR AFFILIATION

Leisure-oriented expressive voluntary organizations attract individuals who seek to both enjoy leisure activities in a group setting and to become more proficient at them. Some outdoor recreation organizations require a demonstrated commitment to the activity which forms the central interest of the group. Thus, the Mazamas, a major outdoor recreation club in Oregon studied by Harry (1967), defines membership eligibility as follows: "any person who has climbed to the summit of a snowpeak on which there is at least one living glacier, the top of which can not be reached by any other means than on foot." According to Harry, membership in the club provides an opportunity for the appreciation of nature, a chance to gain honors and awards for participating in club activities (summit certificates were awarded for climbing mountains), and occasions to get together with other people. In a more instrumentally oriented organization, we would expect such interests to be secondary, and that both the initial attraction to the organization, and the factors which sustain interest in the organization would relate more to the organization's externally directed actions. Our questionnaire included two open-ended questions allowing us to examine this distinction: one dealing with the reasons for initial attraction to the club, and the other inquiring about the reasons for retaining membership in it.

Our data show a definite shift in the reasons for affiliating with the Sierra Club. Puget Sound Group members who joined seven to nine years ago were nearly equally divided between those who affiliated because of opportunities for outdoor experiences and fellowship (43%), and those who saw their membership as a vehicle for increasing their knowledge on conservation issues and for having the club represent them on these issues (45%). In more recent years, however, opportunities for recreation and fellowship have steadily declined as the main reasons for joining the organization: 20.3% of the members of four to six years' standing cited these reasons, as did 9.3% of those joining two to three years ago, and similarly for only 4.5% of the newest members surveyed, those affiliating within a year of the time of the survey. Likewise, consistently larger proportions of the members have joined in recent years because they see the club as a source of information and a vehicle to represent their views on conservation issues: 64.4% of those who joined four to six years ago cited these reasons, as did 70.6% affiliating two to three years ago, and similarly for 72.7% of those joining most recently. Thus, in terms of the reasons for initial membership, the Puget Sound Group is increasingly viewed by its members as an instrumental organization. Rather than expecting their membership to yield the camaraderie and skills growing out of group outdoor experiences, the expressive services so frequently supplied by the Sierra Club in years past, new members tend to be attracted to the club as a source of more comprehensive information on conservation issues and as their voice in instrumental action on these issues.

The shift of Puget Sound Group members to a more instrumental orientation is increasingly apparent when we examine the reasons which members cite for remaining in the club. Depending on how long they have been in the club, between 76.7% and 81.7% reported that they continue their affiliation because of the club's involvement in environmental issues. Not more than 5.2% in any category of member seniority indicated that they renew their membership because of the club's extensive outdoor recreation program, its major expressive function. This finding is particularly striking in view of the fact that 43.3% of those who have been members at least seven years cited expressive factors as their reason for affiliation. The unknown factor, of course, and one which is of substantial import in changing organizations, is whether the increasingly instrumental orientation led other expressively oriented members to withdraw from the club. The orientation of newer members suggests even greater support for instrumental action, and perhaps an increasing strain on those older members who initially joined for more expressive reasons. At the present time, the instrumental orientation held by long-term members, coupled with this same perspective predominating among those joining more recently, suggests that the Puget Sound Group has indeed become a more instrumentally involved environmental organization.

PARTICIPATION IN ORGANIZATIONAL ACTIVITIES AND OUTDOOR RECREATION

Among the many aspects of membership participation, two are of special importance to an analysis of the environmental involvement of outdoor recreation organizations. First is the actual participation of members in the formal structure and activities of the organization. As indicated previously, expressive organizations are characterized by a high level of participation and involvement in organizational decision-making, while instrumental organizations usually exhibit a low degree of direct membership participation. The second aspect relates to actual participation in organized outdoor recreation activities. To the extent that current members of the Puget Sound Group of the Sierra Club still consider themselves "companions on the trail," we would expect a high level of individual participation in a variety of forms of outdoor recreation. However, to the extent that outdoor recreation becomes less linked to the club's instrumental activities, members would not be expected to reflect such a level of participation.

Although the Puget Sound Group has an elaborate committee structure and an executive committee, only 12.6% of the members reported that they have ever served as an officer or committee member, and more than half of those who have served are no longer incumbents. More striking is the members' lack of participation in other club activities, ranging from committee meetings to the annual banquet. Nearly three out of five members (57.2%) indicated that they do not attend club functions, while 31.4% reported that they do so at least once a year, but not monthly. Intensive involvement, at least once a month, was reported by 11.4% of the members. Thus, only a small fraction of the membership appears to be regularly involved in either the administrative structure or the activity program of the group, clearly characteristic of instrumentally rather than of expressively oriented organizations.

When the members' reports of their outdoor recreation activity over the past year are examined, it appears that they do *not* regularly participate in a wide variety of outdoor activities. Though it is not surprising, given the Sierra Club's emphasis on nonconsumptive uses of wilderness, that 92.6% of the members did not hunt during the previous twelve months, they also reported quite infrequent participation in the forms of outdoor recreation one might expect of wilderness-oriented conservationists—e.g., snowshoeing, fishing, wild-river boating, cross-country skiing. Less than a third reported any mountain-climbing trips, and backpacking was mentioned by slightly over half (51.3%) of the respondents. The activity which the greatest portion of the members pursued was hiking, with 76.5% indicating that they had gone on at least one trip during the past year; only half the hikers, however, had done so four or more times during the previous year. Thus, with the exception of hiking, and possibly of backpacking, the members of the Puget Sound Group do not regularly participate in outdoor recreation activities. One would expect both more frequent participation and a wider range of activities on the part of conservation activists whose primary motivation is to derive the expressive rewards found in group-based recreation. In terms of outdoor recreation activity, then, members of the Puget Sound Group exhibit a relatively low level of interest in the expressive enjoyment of the environment.

MEMBERSHIP IN OTHER OUTDOOR RECREATION AND ENVIRONMENTAL ORGANIZATIONS

Additional evidence which suggests that Puget Sound Group members are primarily instrumentally oriented is seen in the types of other groups to which they belong (two-thirds of the respondents reported at least one other group membership). Relatively few (17.1%) are also members of one or more outing clubs, while 24.1% are affiliated with at least one other mixed outing-environmental issue organization. Nearly half, however, belong to one or more exclusively issue-oriented organizations. Thus, of those with other environmental group affiliations, most belong to primarily instrumental environmental organizations, rather than to more expressively oriented outing or mixed outing-environmental issue groups. Moreover, those who are active in the Puget Sound Group tend also to be those who are affiliated with other environmental-issue groups. For example, a third of those who report weekly or monthly activity in the Sierra Club are also members of at least one other local outing-environmental issue group, as compared with 24.5% of those participating in the Sierra Club on an annual basis, and 19.7% of those who report that they never attend Sierra Club activities. Similarly, one-third of the weekly or monthly participants report membership in three or more exclusively instrumental environmental organizations, as compared to less than 10% of all other respondents. Thus, not only are other instrumental organizations generally favored by Puget Sound Group members who have other affiliations, but this relationship is accentuated for those who are regular participants in the Sierra Club group.

SUMMARY AND SUGGESTIONS FOR FUTURE RESEARCH

A preliminary analysis of our data indicates that members of the Puget Sound Group of the Sierra Club are more instrumentally concerned with the quality of the environment than expressively motivated to enjoy the environment through outdoor recreation. Drawn mainly from upper-middle and upper socioeconomic strata, almost all new members are initially attracted to the club out of their instrumental concern for the environment, and long-term members, up to one-half of whom may have originally joined the club for its outdoor program, have now largely shifted their primary concern to the quality and protection of the environment. Relatively few members participate in the governance of the organization or in its other activities, and, with the exception of hiking, and possibly backpacking, most members are not avid outdoor recreation enthusiasts. Finally, for those who also belong to other environmental organizations, most are affiliated with primarily issue-oriented groups, rather than with recreation clubs, with the more active participants in the Sierra Club group more likely to have these additional instrumental affiliations. We surmise, on the basis of these admittedly weak data, that the priorities of the Puget Sound Group members have shifted in recent years from outdoor recreation, mixed with an occasional concern for protecting certain wilderness areas, to an almost exclusive emphasis today on general environmental quality issues, ranging from wilderness protection and outdoor recreation, to urban pollution and population control. The members, in short, are no longer the outdoor recreationists of yesteryear, but rather today's environmental politicos, in the vanguard of society's newest social movement.

But the significance of our findings and conclusions lies neither in their substantive accuracy nor in their methodological adequacy, as much as in the directions they suggest for future research. Rather than examining only outdoor recreationists as persons highly concerned with the environment, as in previous studies, our data indicate that future research must range more widely to include persons who register their commitment to the environment via formal affiliation with appropriate voluntary organizations, rather than necessarily through their own recreation activities. Though the actual expenditure of leisure time in organizational programs, whether instrumental or expressive, may be generally low, as our data suggest, the environmentalists' allocations of time and energy are undoubtedly sporadic, peaking instrumentally, for example, when important issues are being considered in various public forums. Perhaps, like members of volunteer fire departments, the environmentalists stand ready to combat, when necessary, the major threats to environmental quality, but under ordinary circumstances they allow their organizational leaders—the regulars—to man the watchtowers.

But who are the environmentalists, those who care enough to join an environmental organization, if not to regularly participate in its activities? As already mentioned, our respondents may not be typical of Sierra Club members in other parts of the country, as indeed they may not be representative of the entire Puget Sound Group membership, and we strongly doubt that they are typical of environmentalists in general. Our data are consistent with past research in revealing that the environmental movement draws its strength mainly from high socioeconomic strata, but the base of support may now be broadening with the recent rapid growth of the movement. Also, the rather concentrated socioeconomic stations of the environmentalists may only be apparent, stemming from the fact that previous investigations of environmental organizations have focused primarily on major national groups or their more local subunits, and an examination of groups which are not national in scope may indeed reveal a broader socioeconomic base. Whatever the organizations examined, however, and regardless of their members' socioeconomic positions, a more systematic analysis of the questions we have addressed in this paper seems warranted. In addition, future research should extend far beyond an examination of the reasons for the members' original and continuing affiliation, their outdoor recreation preferences and frequency of activity, and the extent of their participation in other organizational functions. Of particular importance, it seems, would be a study of those who belong to a variety of environmental groups. Our data indicate, for example, that approximately two-thirds of the Puget Sound Group members also belong to at least one other environmental organization, and obviously much can be learned about the environmental movement in general from an examination of those with multiple memberships in a variety of related groups. Is there, as our data might suggest, a leadership elite, a relatively small core of highly committed people who devote perhaps almost all of their leisure time to the activities of several organizations? More generally, what is the sequence and etiology of affiliating with numerous environmental groups? Is it a "stepping-stone" process, as speculated by Hendee et al. (1968: 21), where individuals initially join local recreation-related groups and eventually extend their involvement by affiliating with national environmental issue organizations? And finally, to what extent do environmental activists also belong to other nonenvironmental voluntary organizations, such as civil rights groups and fraternal orders? Are they "specialists," confining their concern to largely environmental issues and outdoor recreation, or "generalists," who express a wide range of interests—avocational, political, and vocational—through membership in a variety of voluntary organizations with diverse priorities and goals (Harry et al., 1969)? In short, we are suggesting that future research on individual environmentalists turn away from recreationists in the field, and focus instead on environmentalists in the specific context of their voluntary organizational memberships and in the larger context of their general ideologies and perspectives on life.

But it would be remiss to encourage future research directed only at the members of a variety of environmental groups without emphasizing as well the importance of examining the differences among the organizations themselves. Indeed, the evolution of social movements may be viewed largely in terms of the complex web of voluntary organizations which advocate and oppose the goals of the movement. In the environmental movement, one notes considerable diversity, even among organizations which agree on the desired course of action on a specific environmental issue. Thus far, research has focused on those large national organizations which are in the forefront of the movement. But research must also include local groups, and issue-specific "Save the ... " organizations. Further, relatively few outdoor recreation organizations approach the instrumentality of the Sierra Club. An important area of future research is the "triggering event," which impels the expressive organization into political action, and the impact of success or failure on the future instrumental involvement by the organization. Inability to satisfactorily resolve environmental issues which relate to recreational interests may "radicalize" the organization, along the lines of the residents of Santa Barbara who were continually frustrated in their attempts to "Get Oil Out" (Molotch, 1970).

Analysis of new organizations is especially critical for the understanding of the future of a social movement. Several new organizational forms have already appeared in the environmental movement, such as the statewide or regional environmental council and the national issue-specific coalition (Coalition Against the SST). New forms of outdoor recreation may also be expected to result in voluntary organizations, especially where the activity stimulates the development of a new industry to supply recreational equipment, as in the case of snowmobiling, or requires a special natural setting, as in skin-diving. Some of the organizations, like the National Rifle Association and various ski associations, may include both citizens interested in the enjoyment of outdoor recreation, and those whose livelihood depends on the manufacture of equipment or operation of facilities for recreationists. Finally, there is another type of organization which should be of special interest to those who wish to understand the dynamics of the movement on the level of strategy or tactics. What might be called the "pseudo-citizen" organization may be formed to directly combat environmentalist groups. Externally, pseudo-citizen organizations appear to be spontaneously organized, noneconomic citizens' groups. In fact, however, they may be the result of deliberate action by industries. In Oregon, the timber industry and government officials formed the now-defunct Public Resources Council of Oregon. And in San Francisco, advertising agency employees organized "Artists For The Pyramid" to help their client, the Transamerica Corporation, win approval of a much-criticized office tower (Krizek, 1970).

Another area of needed research relates to the internal dynamics of organizational change. Data which suggest changes among members of groups must be matched by analysis of the behavior of the organization, as reflected in publications and resolutions about environmental issues, committee structure, organizational budgets, and political action. Further, we would expect to find evidence of intraorganizational stress and conflict in many outdoor recreation groups. Stable organizations may have a high degree of congruence between organizational goals, leadership implementation of these goals, and membership support and involvement. But we would expect few of the organizations which are pulled into the environmental movement to reflect such an optimal mix. Rather, analysis of the points of incongruity may yield especially incisive examples of the dynamics of organizational change. Some members may object to "making things all political," while others may forge a strong link between the group's conservation committee and a statewide environmental council. Meetings dedicated to a discussion of the group's strategy for environmental action may disappoint those who came seeking companionship and conversation. And the organization's "politicos" may feel that marching on the Forest Supervisor's office is more important than walking on a back-country trail.

Our future research will focus on these important changes, both on the level of individual members and in terms of organizational behavior. We encourage others to join us in examining what may be the major social movement of the seventies.

NOTES

1. In part, the environmental movement is a direct descendant of the earlier concern with the preservation of the natural environment. The "conservation-preservation" emphasis which led to the formation of the Redwoods and North Cascades National Parks is still seen in attempts to prohibit ocean-dumping of industrial wastes and other practices which have a negative impact on environments which may be far removed from back-country wilderness areas. Roderick Nash (1967) has written one of the best histories of the conservation-preservation movement. For a discussion of the role of one organization in that movement, see Holway Jones' (1965) history of the Sierra Club.

2. Instrumental voluntary associations are those which are designed to maintain or change some normative condition, while expressive associations focus on activities which have no external goal and are primarily for the benefit of members. In instrumental organizations, "members are committed to goals which do not necessarily contribute to their own personal and immediate gratification" (Jacoby and Babchuk, 1963: 462).

3. In this paper, we treat "environmentalist" and "conservationist" as equivalent in meaning. Thus, the "conservation organizations" described in the previous research are referred to as "environmental organizations," since the older label does not adequately describe the new role of these organizations.

REFERENCES

Babchuk, Nicholas and John N. Edwards
    1965 "Voluntary associations and the integration hypothesis." Soc. Inquiry 35 (Spring): 149-167.
Burch, William R., Jr.
    1965 "The play world of camping: research into the social meaning of outdoor recreation." Amer. J. of Sociology 70 (March): 604-612.
    1969 "The social circles of leisure: competing explanations." J. of Leisure Research 1 (Spring): 125-148.

Devall, W. B.
1970a "The governing of a voluntary organization: oligarchy and democracy in the Sierra Club." Ph.D. dissertation. University of Oregon.
1970b "Conservation: an upper-middle class social movement: a replication." J. of Leisure Research 2 (Spring): 123-126.

Harry, Joseph
1967 "Mazamas: who are we? why do we belong?" Mazama: 71-74.

––– Richard P. Gale, and John C. Hendee
1969 "Conservation: an upper-middle class social movement." J. of Leisure Research 1 (Summer): 246-254.

Hendee, John C., Richard P. Gale, and Joseph Harry
1969 "Conservation, politics, and democracy." J. of Soil and Water Conservation 24 (November/December): 212-215.

Hendee, John C., William R. Catton, Larry D. Marlow, and C. Frank Brockman
1968 "Wilderness users in the Pacific Northwest–their characteristics, values, and management preferences." USDA Forest Service Research Paper PNW-61. Portland, Ore.: Forest and Range Experiment Station.

Jacoby, Arthur P. and Nicholas Babchuk
1963 "Instrumental and expressive voluntary associations." Sociology and the Social Research 47 (July): 461-471.

Jones, Holway R.
1965 John Muir and the Sierra Club: The Battle for Yosemite. San Francisco: Sierra Club.

King, David
1966 "Activity patterns of campers." U.S. Forest Service Research Note NC-18. St. Paul, Minn.: North Central Forest Experimental Station.

Krizek, John
1970 "How to build a pyramid: a kit of PR tools helps win San Francisco's approval for a new high-rise office building." Public Relations J. 26 (December): 17-21.

LaPage, Wilbur F.
1967 "Camper characteristics differ at public and commercial campgrounds in New England." U.S. Forest Service Research Note NE-59. Upper Darby, Pa.: Northeast Forest Experiment Station.

Molotch, Harvey
1970 "Oil in Santa Barbara and power in America." Soc. Inquiry 40 (Winter): 131-144.

Nash, Roderick
1967 Wilderness and the American Mind. New Haven: Yale Univ. Press.

ORRRC–Outdoor Recreation Resources Review Commission
1962 "Wilderness and recreation–a report on resources, values, and problems." ORRRC Study Report 3. Washington, D.C.: Government Printing Office.

LEISURE AND MENTAL HEALTH

A Study in a Program of Leisure Research

JOHN NEULINGER

The City College of The City University of New York

The **problem of leisure** has reached a stage where the time for piecemeal, isolated studies has passed. What is needed are long-range, systematic research efforts. Below is an outline of one such program of research, partially in progress and partially only in a planning stage, that attempts to encompass all relevant aspects of the leisure domain, as seen from a sociopsychological viewpoint. In addition, data will be presented from a study that deals with the relationship of leisure attitudes to personality dimensions and mental health.

A PROGRAM OF LEISURE RESEARCH

For purposes of planning individual studies, the leisure domain has been divided into eight areas. These areas are not meant to be mutually exclusive nor are they necessarily exhaustive of all possible research. What is important is that the same kind of research techniques and instruments be used in each area of study so that findings can be meaningfully related

AUTHOR'S NOTE: *This research was supported in part by Grant RF-292, the Russell Sage Foundation. The author is grateful to M. Breit for her helpful comments and suggestions on the manuscript.*

to each other. In this way it is hoped to build up systematic knowledge about leisure behavior which, in turn, can be the basis as well as the testing ground of a sound theory of leisure.

THE CONCEPTUALIZATION OF LEISURE

There is agreement among leisure researchers that there is not a universally accepted definition of the term "leisure" (Clawson, 1964). What is needed, however, is not only a theoretical a priori clarification of the term leisure and related concepts, such as free time, recreation, and work, but also empirical attempts at the delineation of these concepts. Following a research approach suggested by Hanhart (1964), a number of studies have been initiated to delineate the connotative meaning of leisure-related concepts (Neulinger, 1968a). Using a semantic differential (Osgood et al., 1957) as a research tool, profiles of concepts are obtained which are useful in two ways. First, differences and similarities between concepts, like leisure and free time or leisure and work, can be brought to light. Second, differences in the meaning of these concepts to different subgroups of the population can be investigated. Thus, the term leisure may mean different things to professionals, to blue-collar workers, or to housewives.

THE MEASUREMENT OF LEISURE

Two approaches to the measurement of leisure are being followed. In one, the goal is the delineation of basic leisure attitude dimensions. In a preliminary study (Neulinger and Breit, 1969), five dimensions have been identified. A replication study just completed confirmed the stability of these dimensions (Neulinger and Breit, 1971).

A second approach to the measurement of leisure is through the delineation of leisure types. The attempt here is to discover distinct subgroups within the larger population who share common beliefs and attitudes about leisure. Again, the approach is an empirical, not an a priori one. The intention is not to set up theoretical or ideal leisure types and then attempt to fit people into them, but rather to sort out people in terms of similarities and see whether types actually exist. The method used will be a Q-factor analysis which has been used quite successfully for this purpose (see Stein and Neulinger, 1968).

THE DETERMINATION OF PREVAILING LEISURE ATTITUDES

Present leisure research has been characterized as consisting primarily of studies dealing with leisure activities, leisure expenditures of time and money, or leisure meanings (Meyersohn, 1969). The category that needs to be added to this list is leisure attitudes. What do people think, feel, and do about leisure?

COVARIATES OF LEISURE ATTITUDES

Present leisure research has been criticized as being "little else than a reporting of survey data on what selected samples of individuals do with the time in which they are not working and in the correlation of these data with conventional demographic variables" (Berger, 1963). What is planned is the correlation of soundly established leisure dimensions with relevant sociopsychological variables so that hypotheses about the nature, origin, and change of these dimensions may be tested.

THE DEVELOPMENT OF LEISURE ATTITUDES

To ascertain prevailing leisure attitudes is one thing; to investigate how these attitudes develop is another. A knowledge of the covariates of leisure attitudes is certainly helpful to such an enterprise, but to develop an adequate theory of the development of leisure attitudes, specific types of attitude surveys will be required, including longitudinal studies and cross-generation comparisons.

EXPERIMENTAL LEISURE RESEARCH

This is an area of research that is practically barren. Yet once leisure hypotheses have been developed, their validity will have to be tested through laboratory or field experiments. Some recent attempts and suggestions in this direction seem quite promising (Witt and Bishop, 1970).

LEISURE AS A SOCIAL PROBLEM

The primary task is a clarification of what it is about leisure that presents a problem. Is the problem of leisure and the problem of free time one and the same, or are they different problems? Does leisure present the same problem to all people? If not, what are the specific problems for specific groups of people? Is it correct to assume that work has lost its potential for self-definition, and is leisure taking the place of work? How do the person's work and leisure attitudes relate to his personality integration? A study relating to this question is reported in the second section of this paper.

THE PROMOTION OF LEISURE

Freely admitting a biased judgment—namely, the recognition of leisure as a social good—ways of promoting it need to be studied. If the problem of leisure is seen as the problem of free time, research efforts ought to center around the proper utilization of free time. If, however, the problem of leisure is seen as a problem of self-actualization and alienation from work, the concern will be with providing more meaningful activities for people. In either case, some educational process will have to be developed, the most important goal of which would be the creation of an atmosphere that would at least equate the value of leisure with that of work.

This concludes the discussion of a general program of leisure research. Following is the presentation of a study carried out within the larger context of the total program.

LEISURE ATTITUDES AND MENTAL HEALTH

A frequently expressed opinion is that too much leisure (that is, free time) is bad. Part of this sentiment may be traced to the Protestant ethic. However, this view also seems to reflect the assumption that most people are incapable of coping with too much free time. For example, the Group for the Advancement of Psychiatry states in one of its official publications (1958): "for many Americans leisure is dangerous," and it substantiates its claim by referring to the common clinical entity, "Sunday neurosis." The inability of the person to cope with his free time is related to his lack of inner resources and adaptability to a new environment—that is, a work-free existence. The characteristics quoted here, inner resources, environmental mastery and so forth, are the very criteria which are often used to define mental health (for example, Jahoda, 1958; Hartmann, 1964). Thus, we suspect that the way in which a person thinks and feels about leisure will be related to his state of mental health.

In this study, an attempt is made to establish relationships between a norm of mental health and basic leisure attitudes. One of the major problems in such an enterprise is the fact that no totally satisfactory measure of mental health exists (Offer and Sabshin, 1966). However, a measure has recently been developed which can be used to give any person a score reflecting his closeness to a general norm of mental health (Neulinger, 1968b; Neulinger et al., 1970). The instrument used to obtain this measure also provides information about the person's relative position on twenty personality variables. The purpose of the present study, then, is to examine whether leisure attitudes are related to the person's personality structure and particularly to his closeness to a norm of mental health. No predetermined hypotheses were tested, and the research was purely explorative.

METHOD

SUBJECTS

The sample was a subsample of a larger study and consisted of 81 adults working full-time—46 males and 35 females. Their mean age was 37.9 years, ranging from 18 to 67. Fifteen (19%) indicated as their religious preference Protestant, 13 (16%) Catholic, 34 (42%) Jewish, 18 (22%) none, and one (1%) other. The subjects' marital status was 26 (32%) single, 49 (60%) married, and the balance separated, divorced, or widowed. Their median educational level was "some college," ranging from 6 (7%) with 11 or fewer years of education, to 26 (32%) with 17 or more years. Family income was equally high; median income about $13,000, ranging from 6 subjects with incomes from $5,001 to $7,000, to 17 subjects with incomes of $20,000 or more. There was a wide range of occupations, including the professions, business, industry, and the trades. The sample thus is atypical, in that it has a predominance of Jewish subjects, and is relatively high in terms of both educational and income levels.

QUESTIONNAIRES

Two questionnaires were administered. One, "A Study of Leisure," contained, in addition to socioeconomic questions, 32 items used to derive 5 factor dimensions: (1) affinity to leisure, (2) society's role in leisure planning, (3) self-definition through leisure or work, (4) amount of perceived leisure, (5) amount of work or vacation desired (Neulinger and Breit, 1969). It also included a semantic differential (Osgood et al., 1957) consisting of 16 adjective pairs associated with the concepts leisure and work. The second questionnaire was the "Stein Self-Description questionnaire" (Stein, 1966; Stein and Neulinger, 1968), which consists of 20 paragraphs each describing one of Murray's (1938) manifest needs. In responding to the questionnaire, the subject is asked to rank the paragraphs from the one which is most descriptive of himself (rank of 1) to the one which is least descriptive of himself (rank of 20).

NORM OF MENTAL HEALTH

The norms of mental health used were profiles of the male and female optimally integrated person (OIP) as perceived by 114 United States mental health personnel, mostly psychotherapists (Neulinger, 1968b; Neulinger et al., 1970). The profiles were obtained by having the therapists rank the 20 paragraphs in Stein's Self-Description questionnaire from most descriptive of the OIP (rank 1) to least descriptive (rank 20). Each therapist furnished both a male and a female OIP profile.

A correlation coefficient between each individual's 20 need self-description profiles and the respective male or female OIP profile was used as a measure of his mental health, that is, his closeness to the OIP. This closeness measure, ranging from +1.00 for maximum closeness, to −1.00 for minimal closeness, will be referred to as the "Mental Health Index" (MHI).

PROCEDURE

Questionnaires were distributed by the City College students to adults working full-time, within the context of a larger survey on leisure attitudes. Anonymity of respondents and a minimum of pressure were maintained to avoid false responses.

RESULTS

As shown in Table 1, there were a number of significant correlations among the five leisure attitude dimensions and personality variables. A separate analysis for males and females showed that most of these relationships were quite sex-specific. For example, the dimension of society's role in leisure planning

TABLE 1

**SIGNIFICANT PERSONALITY CORRELATES OF FIVE
LEISURE DIMENSIONS, CONTROLLED FOR SEX OF
RESPONDENT (correlation coefficients)**

Dimensions	Total Group (n=81)	Males (n=46)	Females (n=35)
Affinity to leisure			
n-deference	-.23[a]	-.20	-.29
n-sentience	.22[a]	.19	.27
n-order	-.17	.11	-.55[b]
Society's role in leisure planning			
n-order	.25[a]	.13	.37[a]
n-nurturance	.25[a]	.36[a]	.12
n-aggression	-.19	-.39[b]	.13
Self-definition through leisure or work			
n-achievement	-.30[b]	-.23	-.47[b]
n-defendance	.33[b]	.37[a]	.24
-n-counteraction	-.27[a]	-.13	-.47[b]
Amount of perceived leisure			
n-sentience	.27[a]	.26	.31
n-exhibition	.27[a]	.17	.31
n-infavoidance	-.14	-.03	-.40[a]
n-deference	-.14	-.02	-.34[a]
n-achievement	-.17	-.31[a]	-.13
Amount of work or vacation desired			
n-exhibition	.27[a]	.17	.31
n-abasement	-.09	.11	-.34[a]
n-affiliation	.19	.30[a]	.06
n-autonomy	-.14	-.32[a]	.02

a. $p < .05$
b. $p < .01$

is positively related to need order; note, however, that this relationship is accounted for by the females in the group, not the males. On the other hand, need nurturance is positively related to and need aggression negatively related to the same dimension, but only in terms of the male respondents. Similarly, only for females, there is a negative relationship between self-definition through leisure or work and both need achievement and need counteraction. Another striking example is the negative relationship between the dimension of affinity to leisure and need order, which again holds only for the female respondents.

None of the five leisure dimensions correlated significantly with the MHI for either the total group or for males and females analyzed separately. The absence of significant relationships could mean (a) that we used inadequate measuring devices, (b) that there was too much noise in the data—i.e., that given the relatively small number of subjects, the effects of other variables overshadowed those related to the mental health of the respondents—or (c) that, indeed, one's degree of mental health is independent of and unrelated to one's position on the five leisure dimensions. It remains for future studies to determine which of these alternatives is the valid one.

The MHI did relate to the respondents' perception of the concept of leisure (Table 2). Interestingly enough, the concept of work was totally unrelated to the MHI. Findings indicate that the respondent who has a high MHI rating saw leisure as full rather than empty, and as refreshing rather than tiring. Separate male/female analyses again revealed sex-specific relationships. The well-integrated male respondent tended to see leisure as sociable rather than solitary, and as necessary rather

TABLE 2

**MENTAL HEALTH AND THE PERCEPTION OF LEISURE:
SIGNIFICANT CORRELATIONS BETWEEN THE *OIP* INDEX
AND ADJECTIVE PAIRS ON A SEMANTIC DIFFERENTIAL,
CONTROLLED FOR SEX OF RESPONDENT**

Leisure is . . .		Total Group (n=81)	Males (n=46)	Females (n=35)
(1)	(7)			
empty ————— full		.35[b]	.34[a]	.36[a]
refreshing ————tiring		-.35[b]	-.32[a]	-.37[a]
solitary ————— sociable		.26[a]	.30[a]	.09
necessary ——————unnecessary		-.27[a]	-.37[a]	-.11
meaningful ——————meaningless		-.22[a]	-.10	-.50[b]
valuable ——————worthless		-.21	-.16	-.30
good —————bad		-.18	-.06	-.46[b]
pleasant ————— unpleasant		-.11	.05	-.48[b]

a. $p < .05$
b. $p < .01$

than unnecessary. The well-integrated female saw leisure as meaningful rather than meaningless, good rather than bad, and pleasant rather than unpleasant. As indicated above, none of the adjective pairs related significantly to the concept of work.

DISCUSSION

The purpose of this study was to investigate the relationship of personality characteristics and a measure of mental health to previously identified leisure dimensions. In addition, the question was raised whether persons of varying degrees of mental health might have different conceptions of work and leisure.

Our measure of mental health did not relate to any of the leisure attitude dimensions. We suggested three alternative explanations for the absence of significant relationships, but we really favor the second one, that there was too much noise in the data. There are clearly a number of critical variables which must be taken into account before we can expect to get at the true relationships involved. One of these would be the person's occupation; another equally important one might be the person's satisfaction with his occupation. Unfortunately, our small sample size made such further subanalyses inappropriate. We are presently collecting data on a sample of 800 adults which should enable us to carry out more thorough analyses.

The relationships described in Table 1 among leisure attitudes and personality needs do throw some light on the kind of person who might hold one view rather than another. Keeping in mind that what follows are mere speculations, we may well accept that a person who has an affinity to leisure—i.e., who is willing to see himself spending a life of leisure—is one who is not too conforming or too deferent to others who might hold a different view. Such a person would be thought of as being concerned with pleasure and the enjoyment of life. How do we account for the relatively high (−.55) relationship of need order to affinity to leisure, for female respondents only? A scatter plot of the 35 respondents involved revealed that this relationship is not an artifact brought about by one or two extreme scores, but that it reflects a trend prevailing for the majority of respondents. The working female, who is high in need order, does not care for the life of leisure, while the one low in need order shows a much greater affinity for such a life. We might account for this by associating order with work and the lack of order or restrictions with leisure. Why does this relationship hold only for females? We have no ready answer at this point, but it may be worth noting that it is also the female high in need order, and not the male, who is in favor of assigning society a role in leisure-planning. Perhaps this type of respondent tries to overcome the feeling of discomfort she experiences due to the relatively unstructured nature of leisure by having society provide the desired controls. Note further that it is the female high in need achievement, high in need counteraction, and low in need abasement who defines herself through work rather than leisure. In contrast, the male who favors assigning society a role in leisure-planning seems to be doing so because he cares, because he wants to be helpful, and not because he needs to act out his aggressive impulses. If the male defines himself through leisure rather than through work, he finds himself in need of defending this still unpopular position.

We shall refrain from trying to account for all significant relationships, realizing that some of these may be chance factors and may disappear upon replication. We do feel, however, that these data represent at least a tentative base for future comparisons and cross-validations.

Let us now turn to the final question, the relationship of mental health to the conceptions of work and leisure. The fact that the person's conception of work was unrelated to his state of mental health, while his view of leisure varied as a function of his personality integration confirms our basic belief that leisure is an ideal area in which to study personality dynamics. For most people, work is constricted, defined, and routine. Leisure, in contrast, is open, unrestricted, undefined. "In our leisure we stand exposed" (Kaplan, 1960). What a man will do with his leisure is largely up to him. The fact that the well-integrated person finds his leisure full and refreshing only confirms that he is a well-integrated person. We shall refrain from offering explanations for the sex differences found, until these findings can be validated in further studies.

In summary, we would like to place this study into the context of our larger program of leisure research. As an isolated study, the findings reported here are tenuous. The sample size is small, and the relationships discovered are relatively weak. However, in connection with related studies being carried on now and planned in the near future, these findings will take on more meaning as they are either confirmed or disconfirmed. Our hope is that other researchers will join in on the investigation of the problems outlined in the first section of this paper so that we may achieve an integrated research effort into the problems of leisure.

REFERENCES

Berger, Bennett M.
> 1963 "The sociology of leisure." Pp. 21-40 in E. O. Smigel (ed.) Work and Leisure. New Haven, Conn.: College and University Press.

Clawson, Marion
> 1964 "How much leisure, now and in the future?" In J. J. Charlesworth (ed.) Leisure in America: Blessing or Curse? Philadelphia: American Academy of Political and Social Science.

Group for the Advancement of Psychiatry
> 1958 "The psychiatrist's interest in leisure-time activities." Report 39. New York.

Hanhart, Dieter
> 1964 Arbeiter in der Freizeit. Bern, Switzerland: Hans Huber.

Hartmann, Heinz
> 1964 Essays on Ego Psychology. New York: International Universities Press.

Jahoda, Marie
> 1958 "Current concepts of positive mental health." Monograph Series 1. New York: Basic Books.

Kaplan, Max
> 1960 Leisure in America: A Social Inquiry. New York: John Wiley.

Meyersohn, Rolf
    1969 "The sociology of leisure in the United States: introduction and bibliography, 1945-1965." J. of Leisure Research 1 (Winter): 53-68.
Murray, Henry A. et al.
    1938 Explorations in Personality. New York: Oxford Univ. Press.
Neulinger, John
    1968a "An investigation of leisure." Progress Report 1. City College, New York, N.Y.
    1968b "Perceptions of the optimally integrated person: a redefinition of mental health." Proceedings of the Seventy-sixth Annual Convention, APA 2: 553-554.
— — — and Miranda Breit
    1969 "Attitude dimensions of leisure." J. of Leisure Research 1 (Summer): 255-261.
— — — and Miranda Breit
    1971 "Attitude dimensions of leisure: a replication." J. of Leisure Research 3 (Spring): 108-115.
Neulinger, John, Morris Stein, Morton Schillinger, and Joan Welkowitz
    1970 "Perceptions of the optimally integrated person as a function of therapists' characteristics." Perceptual and Motor Skills 30 (April): 375-384.
Offer, Daniel and Melvin Sabshin
    1966 Normality, Theoretical and Clincal Concepts of Mental Health. New York: Basic Books.
Osgood, Charles E., George J. Suci, and Percy H. Tannenbaum
    1957 The Measurement of Meaning. Urbana: Univ. of Illinois Press.
Stein, Morris I.
    1966 Volunteers for Peace. New York: John Wiley.
— — — and John Neulinger
    1968 "A typology of self-descriptions." Pp. 390-403 in M. M. Katz, J. O. Cole, and W. E. Barton (eds.) The Role and Methodology of Classification in Psychiatry and Psychopathology. Washington, D.C.: Government Printing Office.
Witt, Peter A., and Doyle W. Bishop
    1970 "Situational antecedents to leisure behavior." J. of Leisure Research 2 (Winter): 64-77.

WORK AND LEISURE
Situational Attitudes

JOSEPH HARRY
Wayne State University

Some years ago, Robert Dubin (1956: 131-132) advanced "the axiom that social experience is inevitably segmented" for most individuals in industrial society, "with each social segment lived out more or less independently of the rest." The worlds of work and leisure are psychologically separate. His research led to the conclusion that attitudes toward work and leisure are situationally specific. Thus, the modern industrial worker does not tend to seek primary affective gratification in work situations, nor does he apply criteria of technological appropriateness or efficiency when engaged in family and leisure activities. By implication, the main links between the worlds of work and of leisure are those of structural constraints—i.e., time availability, time distribution, resources, and the like.

Although Dubin argued both that work interests were independent of leisure interests and that leisure interests were independent of work interests, his research explored mainly the former linkage. Thus, looking at factory workers, it was reported that "the workplace is not very congenial to the development of preferred informal human relationships" (Dubin,

AUTHOR'S NOTE: *Acknowledgments for financial support for this paper are due the Pacific Northwest Forest and Range Experiment Station, U.S. Forest Service.*

1956: 136). However, the application by workers of work-based attitudes to nonwork situations was not explored. Accordingly, it remains possible that attitudes generated at the workplace may be generalized to nonwork situations. Such a hypothesis has been put forward by Miller and Swanson (1958) in their attempts to show the effects on child-rearing practices of parental involvement in bureaucratic versus entrepreneurial work organizations. Below, we explore this second part of the work-leisure independence hypothesis.

THE NATURAL ENVIRONMENT: WORKPLACE OR PLAYGROUND?

The above attitudinal independence hypothesis has been formulated on a more concrete level by workers in the fields of leisure research and outdoor recreation. In his review of the literature on rural-urban differences in outdoor recreation, Hendee (1969: 337) describes a hypothesis that the differences in attitudes toward the natural environment may be due to differences in types of occupation. "Since rural occupations such as farming, mining, and logging are typically based on the exploitation and consumption of natural resources, they might encourage an exploitative attitude toward natural resources," thus allowing a generalization of workplace attitudes to outdoor recreational leisure situations. "Urban occupations, on the other hand, are typically in manufacturing or service industries far removed from the natural environment. Urban residence may thus allow the development of appreciative attitudes towards nature," although not necessarily demanding such attitudes. "A utilitarian attitude toward nature may thus be associated with 'harvesting' recreational activities—fishing, hunting, and the like—whereas an appreciative orientation is more closely linked to the realization of aesthetic and social values in outdoor activities" (Hendee, 1969: 337).

In the light of the above discussion of types of occupations associated with rural or urban residence, we advance the following hypotheses:

(1) Persons having occupations which require the direct exploitation of natural resources—farming, mining, logging—will have more exploitative attitudes toward nature than those having other occupations. This hypothesis covers those cases in which work and leisure situations have important aspects in common—as with nature-exploitative occupations and outdoor recreation—and as such asserts that these individuals will have a more extractive and manipulatory attitude toward natural resources in their leisure situations.

(2) Persons having nature-exploitative occupations will look upon outdoor recreational situations as being less appropriate for the expression of social and aesthetic values than those having non-nature-exploitative occupations. This hypothesis argues that, by virtue of its status within the workplace as a resource, the natural environment will serve less as a vehicle for the expression of the social and aesthetic values which are customarily expressed in leisure situations. Rather, to the extent that individuals of nature-exploitative occupations engage in outdoor recreational activities, they will do so in a more exploitative capacity, as stated in hypothesis (1). These two hypotheses constitute, on a relatively concrete level, alternative hypotheses to Dubin's more abstractly formulated independence proposition.

RESEARCH PROCEDURES

Dubin's original subjects were participants in factory work. Ours are participants in leisure activities based upon utilization of the natural environment. The data to be presented come from some 2,412 summer recreation visitors to three national forests and two national parks in the state of Washington. It was necessary to use four different procedures to compile populations from which to sample outdoor recreationists. Wilderness campers, those hiking to remote areas away from roads in the national forests, were sampled from self-registration cards which visitors must complete at trailheads when entering such areas.

National park wilderness campers were sampled from fire permit registrations required of all hikers planning cooking or campfires. These procedures entail some bias, since not all visitors register. Self-registration stations have been found to be 70 to 85% complete, with nonresponse concentrated among horse users, fishermen, solitary hikers, and frequent or long-term users of the area; however, nonresponse is unrelated to occupation or area (Wenger, 1964; Wenger and Gregersen, 1964). It seems reasonable that fire permit registrations in remote areas of national parks operate under similar biases and, thus, these two sets of data are comparable for purposes of the present study. National park car campers were sampled from a list of license numbers recorded by park rangers in eight campgrounds on twelve separate days—three sets of Tuesdays and Wednesdays and three sets of Fridays and Saturdays. National forest car campers were sampled from a list of license numbers recorded on registration cards required of all campers possessing federal area (Golden Eagle) camping permits, which included 75% of the users based upon observational checks. Names and addresses to match the appropriate vehicle license numbers were obtained through the cooperation of many state departments of motor vehicles.

A thirteen-page questionnaire was sent to persons systematically sampled from the populations recorded in each of the four types of areas. The questionnaire requested the usual demographic data plus "like or dislike" responses to a large number of items describing features of the areas, possible activities within the areas, and equipment or facilities the recreationist might like to use or have when in such areas. The response rate was 55.5%, providing a usable sample size of 2,412. This moderate rate of return is attributed to the length of the questionnaire and the fact that the mailings were made during the Christmas holidays.

For purposes of scale construction, eighty of the questionnaire items were factor analyzed using an orthogonal, principal axes solution with varimax rotation and unities as estimates of the communalities. Due to varying completeness of response from item to item, a correlation matrix was first produced with a floating N varying from 2,304 to 2,411. This correlation matrix was then factor analyzed to produce six interpretable factors. Of the six factors extracted, the five germane to our present purposes were utilized as dependent variables in the form of unweighted summated scales. The first two (below) serve as tests of hypothesis (1), the rest as tests of hypothesis (2). The five factors are:

(1) Economic utilization, a sixteen-item scale measuring the extent to which subjects believe that natural resources should be maximally exploited for economic purposes, rather than used for recreational-aesthetic ones.

(2) Freedom, a five-item scale reflecting a desire for unrestrained freedom to practice backwoodsmanly skills, e.g., "putting nails in trees for utensils, cut brush, limbs, or trees for campfire fuel."[1]

(3) Resortism, a twelve-item scale measuring the extent to which recreationists desire developed facilities of a very civilized nature replete with amenities.

(4) Primevalism, a sixteen-item scale reflecting the extent to which subjects desire to participate in recreational activities in a pristine environment showing little evidence of human progress; this factor is largely an aesthetic one.

(5) Gregariousness, a five-item scale reflecting a desire to use the natural environment as a situation for satisfying social motives.

RESULTS

Comparisons of individuals in nature-exploitative and non-exploitative occupations on the five variables listed above are presented in Table 1.

The differences on Economic Utilization and Freedom seem to clearly support hypothesis (1). Subjects with nature-exploitative occupations give economic primacy to the use of natural resources and, to the extent that such resources are seen as appropriate for leisure activities, approach them with an

TABLE 1

MEAN ATTITUDE SCORES ON FIVE VARIABLES
BY OCCUPATIONAL TYPE

| | Occupational Type | | | | | | | |
| | Nature-Exploitative | | Nonex-ploitative | | | | | |
Variable	$\bar{x}$	s.d.	$\bar{x}$	s.d.	t	p^a	n_1^b	n_2
Economic utilization	3.08	0.73	2.58	0.67	8.13	.01	151	2098
Freedom	15.87	3.88	14.69	3.49	3.96	.01	150	2065
Resortism	3.46	1.23	3.31	1.17	1.48	ns	150	2106
Primevalism	7.84	0.88	7.92	0.79	-1.10	ns	151	2110
Gregariousness	13.89	5.30	12.87	5.30	2.21	.03	143	2036

a. Two-tailed .05 tests. The reader may wonder about the use of directional hypotheses together with two-tailed tests. The choice of a one-tailed test implies great confidence in the hypotheses, indeed, obviousness of the hypotheses. Since this state rarely is justified in sociology, this researcher prefers two-tailed tests.

b. The N's fluctuate slightly from item to item due to variable completeness of response.

attitude of *homo faber*. With regard to those variables bearing on hypothesis (2) only Gregariousness showed a significant difference.

With regard to the somewhat mixed results on the variables relating to hypothesis (2), we institute a control for education. Earlier work has shown education to be a major correlate of attitudes toward the natural environment, of having conservationist attitudes and behavior (Harry et al., 1969) and of leisure tastes more generally (Wilensky, 1964). Also, within the factor analysis described earlier, education was found to load −.02, −.47, and −.09 on Economic Utilization, Gregariousness, and Freedom, respectively. Given the loadings on the latter two variables, and given that many of our persons in nature-exploitative occupations are of relatively low education, we explore the possibility that education may be the variable operative here. Table 2 presents Freedom and Gregariousness by occupational type, with education controlled.[2]

As Table 2 shows, the difference on Gregariousness vanishes when educational level is controlled, the latter variable ap-

TABLE 2
MEAN ATTITUDE SCORES ON TWO DEPENDENT
VARIABLES BY OCCUPATIONAL TYPE WITH
LEVEL OF EDUCATION CONTROLLED

| Variable | Occupational Type | | | | | | | |
| | Nature-Exploitative | | Nonex-ploitative | | | | | |
	x	s.d.	x	s.d.	t	p^a	n_1	n_2
Education Gregariousness								
0-12 years	15.08	5.12	14.61	5.40	0.72	ns	75	699
13 years	12.57	5.22	11.94	5.01	1.02	ns	68	1328
Freedom								
0-12 years	15.99	3.79	14.71	3.50	3.07	.01	80	711
13 years	15.74	4.01	14.67	3.50	2.47	.02	70	1345

a. Two-tailed .05 tests.

parently being the major predictor of Gregariousness. Thus, hypothesis (2) seems to find no support at all. What does appear to be supported is Dubin's idea concerning the situational independence of affective and occupational lives. The fact that individuals in nature-exploitative occupations spend their work-lives in the context of the natural environment does not appear to prejudice the extent to which they may see the same environment as an appropriate situation for the satisfaction of primary interests.

As Table 2 also shows, the difference on Freedom does not vanish with the introduction of a control for education. Thus we may conclude that, where work and leisure situations have similar or overlapping features, there may be some transfer of attitudes or skills from the former to the latter, wherein leisure activities become Symbolic Labor, producing various "products" or trophies.[3] Several writers in the area of work and leisure have reported such a transfer of skills from an occupational to a leisure context. Gerstl (1961) observed such differences in his comparisons of advertising men, professors, and dentists. Earlier, Clarke (1956: 303) reported data showing that skilled manual workers engage disproportionately in handicraft hobbies. Quite recently, Burdge (1969: 273) reported, "Hobbies that require a special occupational skill, such as woodworking and automobiles, were common to the prestige levels that include skilled workers. Finally, hobbies that have a daily functional application were common to persons in the lowest prestige groups." Accordingly, it is suggested that there is some direct transfer of occupational culture to the leisure situation.[4]

SUMMARY

It has above been attempted to determine if there are any transfers of attitudes from the workplace to the leisure situation by looking at individuals whose work and leisure environments seem very similar. Consistent with Dubin's earlier findings, there appears to be no relationship between occupation and leisure attitudes when examining locational preferences for satisfaction of primary sociable motives. Thus, there seems to be two-way independence of workplace and leisure-place. Although occupational type was found to be lacking in effect upon the purely *social* content of leisure attitudes, there appeared to be some transfer of *cultural* content. The type of material transferred, however, appears to be relatively specific and technological.

NOTES

1. This factor is quite comparable to that isolated by Burch (1965) called "Symbolic Labor" or *homo faber*. However, our factor also contains an emphasis on freedom from the restraints of civilization, an aspect which he, understandably, could not detect, since his data came largley from observations rather than from subject introspections.

2. Given the gross inequality of the N's involved, rather than using a more elegant analysis of variance technique, we opted for elaboration coupled with t-test in accordance with a suggestion of Blalock's (1960: 264).

3. Further supporting this Symbolic Labor interpretation is the fact that our nature-exploitative subjects report more hunting than the others—56 versus 37% hunt (df = 1, X^2 = 44.49). However, this datum is only suggestive, since the variables of education and proximity to game may be operative here. Thus, behavior is not necessarily a good predictor of attitudes.

4. A possible alternative interpretation of our Freedom variable, emphasizing the freedom aspect more than the skill one, is that differences on this variable support a polarization hypothesis under which individuals engaged in very routine and frustrating work display unlicensed and explosive behavior during their leisure time

(Riesman and Bloomberg, 1957). However, it would appear much more likely under this interpretation that differences would appear between educational levels rather than occupational types. Table 2 shows none.

REFERENCES

Blalock, H. M.
  1960   Social Statistics. New York: McGraw-Hill.
Burch, William R.
  1965   "The playworld of camping: research into the social meaning of outdoor recreation." Amer. J. of Sociology 70 (March): 604-612.
Burdge, Rabel J.
  1969   "Levels of occupational prestige and leisure activity." J. of Leisure Research 1 (Summer): 262-274.
Clarke, Alfred C.
  1956   "Leisure and occupational prestige." Amer. Soc. Rev. 21 (June): 301-307.
Dubin, Robert
  1956   "Industrial workers' worlds: a study of the 'central life interests' of industrial workers." Social Problems 3 (January): 131-142.
Gerstl, Joel E.
  1961   "Leisure, taste, and occupational milieu." Social Problems 9 (Summer): 56-68.
Harry, Joseph, Richard P. Gale, and John C. Hendee
  1969   "Conservation: an upper-middle class social movement." J. of Leisure Research 1 (Summer): 246-254.
Hendee, John C.
  1969   "Rural-urban differences reflected in outdoor recreation participation." J. of Leisure Research 1 (Autumn): 333-342.
Miller, Daniel and Guy E. Swanson
  1958   The Changing American Parent. New York: John Wiley.
Riesman, David and Warner Bloomberg, Jr.
  1957   "Work and leisure: fusion and polarity?" Pp. 69-85 in Conrad Arensberg et al. (eds.) Research in Industrial Human Relations: A Critical Appraisal. New York: Harper.
Wenger, Wiley D.
  1964   "A test of unmanned registration stations on wilderness trails: factors influencing effectiveness." U.S. Forest Service Research Paper PNW-16. Portland, Ore.: Pacific Northwest Forest and Range Experiment Station.
——— and H. M. Gregersen
  1964   "The effect of nonresponse on representativeness of wilderness-trail register information." U.S. Forest Service Research Paper PNW-17. Portland, Ore.: Pacific Northwest Forest and Range Experiment Station.
Wilensky, Harold L.
  1964   "Mass society and mass culture: interdependence or independence?" Amer. Soc. Rev. 29 (April): 173-197.

THE IMPACT OF WORK
ON LEISURE
Toward a Paradigm and
Research Strategy

THOMAS M. KANDO
WORTH C. SUMMERS
Sacramento State College

While much of the literature on the sociology of leisure consists of descriptions of the nonwork activities of various subgroups, it is no longer true that the sociology of leisure is entirely lacking in explanatory studies. Nevertheless, a systematic sociology of leisure has not yet been attempted. One promising explanatory approach which has received wide attention attempts to relate nonwork activity to that portion of the social structure with which it is most often paired conceptually—work. Although those who have dealt with the relationship frequently make common assumptions about how work affects nonwork, few have attempted to explicate the relationship or to research it systematically.

Three related problems, which have obscured the effect of work on leisure, must be resolved before an adequate theory of the relationship between work and nonwork is likely to be developed. The first of these has been the failure to clearly isolate the relationship between work and nonwork from the effects of other confounding variables. The second has been the widespread failure to distinguish between the *meanings* of work and nonwork and the *forms* of work and nonwork. These two

AUTHOR'S NOTE: *This paper was presented at the annual meetings of the Pacific Sociological Association, Honolulu, Hawaii, April 8-10, 1971.*

difficulties lead to a third problem. Discussions of the relationship between work and leisure divide into what Wilensky (1960) has labeled the compensatory and spillover hypotheses. These hypotheses propose that nonwork activity may either compensate for work deprivations or be influenced by characteristics that have spilled over from work. But since the relationship between work and leisure has not been isolated from the influence of other variables, and since the meanings and forms of work and leisure have often been confused, the conditions under which spillover and compensation take place have not been specified. The result is that the compensatory and spillover hypotheses are potentially contradictory.

DIFFICULTIES IN RELATING WORK TO LEISURE

CONFOUNDING WITH OTHER VARIABLES

The first obstacle to a clear understanding of how work affects leisure has been the failure to separate the effects of other variables. Thus the relationship between work and nonwork has often been confounded when demographic indicators correlated with work, such as occupational prestige, social class, subcultures, ethnicity, sex, and age are related to leisure. For example, studies have related particular leisure activities to occupational prestige (Clarke, 1956), to general occupational types such as blue-collar workers (Gordon and Anderson, 1964) and to professionals (Wilensky, 1964). Further, the meaning of leisure has been related to various occupational categories (Riesman, 1958). The subculture of the working class is said to affect their leisure patterns (Gordon and Anderson, 1964) while the middle class dominates community cultural, intellectual, and organizational participation (Reissman, 1954). The forms and meanings of the social life of ethnic subcultures have been described (Myrdal, 1944; Frazier, 1957). Sex has been related to leisure forms and their social-psychological meanings (Stone, 1955; Stone and Taves, 1956) and age has been related to problems of forced leisure upon retirement

(Friedmann and Havighurst, 1954) and to the functions which leisure ought to perform in the absence of work (Havighurst, 1960; Kaplan, 1960b).

Work has also been related to important nonwork activities within a larger theoretical context that includes cultural and societal variables. For example, whether certain kinds of work lead to participation in mass political movements depends on the relationships between societal elites and nonelites (Kornhauser, 1959); while the type of industrializing elite (Kerr et al., 1960), and existing value systems (Lipset, 1961-1962) determine types of trade union behavior. Patterns of consumption and leisure for various occupational groups may depend upon existing values (Weber, 1958), social class (Veblen, 1899), and on the standardizing of mass institutions such as education and the media (Wilensky, 1964).

Any theory dealing with the effect of work on nonwork must account for the influence of such confounding variables and needs to be linked to theories of political sociology, collective behavior, mass society, and stratification which encompass such variables. But it is precisely because work occurs as a critical independent or intervening variable in so many of these theories that we need to clearly specify both the effects that work has on nonwork and the effects that other variables have on the work/nonwork relationship.

CONFUSION BETWEEN FORM AND MEANING

The second obstacle to a systematic theory relating work to nonwork has been the widespread tendency to overlook the complexity of the possible relationships between the outward appearances, or *forms* of work and leisure, and the way they are experienced and interpreted by participants in them, their underlying significance or *meaning;* that is, whether they are sources of sociability, creativity, tension release, or some form of alienation. All compensatory hypotheses assume that when individuals experience some facet of work as a deprivation, they will choose some nonwork activity to compensate for the deprivation; in short, they propose that work affects leisure *because* of the underlying meaning of each. Despite the frequent attempts to link work and leisure through their joint meanings, we are not aware of any attempts to derive common dimensions of meaning for work and leisure from the rich literature on this subject.[1] Problems of interpreting and testing compensatory hypotheses arise when one ignores the possibility that *similar* forms of work or nonwork have *different* meanings for various individuals participating in them or, conversely, that *different* forms may have similar underlying meanings. The mistake most researchers make when using a compensatory hypothesis is to assume that a given type of compensation will occur within only one or a limited number of work or nonwork forms. For example, isolation at work should be compensated for by participation in voluntary associations (Hagedorn and Labovitz, 1968). But if compensation can occur in a number of different nonwork activities besides voluntary associations—family or friendship groups, for example—then the general compensatory hypothesis may be mistakenly rejected. If, on the other hand, similar nonwork activities can mean different things—for some, sociability; for others, achievement or recognition—then compensatory hypotheses may be mistakenly accepted.

Confusion resulting from letting the form of work or nonwork behavior stand for its underlying meaning is made worse because, as already indicated, variables correlated with work—such as occupation, class, ethnicity, subculture, and age, as well as cultural and social conditions—strongly shape nonwork *forms* and thus may further mask compensatory mechanisms. Additional masking may also occur through the standardization of mass leisure activities.

COMPENSATION AND SPILLOVER POTENTIALLY CONTRADICTORY

Quite similar explanations for how work affects leisure appear repeatedly in the literature, although authors differ in how explicitly they express them. Wilensky (1960) has conveniently labeled these the compensatory and spillover hypotheses.

For example, compensatory hypotheses are implicitly employed in the suggestion that workers on automated assembly lines may require less recuperation as their work demands less physical effort, that they may seek creative nonwork outlets because their work is noncreative, and that job isolation may lead them to increased leisure time spent with others (Faunce, 1959); we find it also in the argument that for white-collar workers, "leisure time . . . [may come] to mean an unserious freedom from the authoritarian seriousness of the job" (Mills, 1956: 236).

Two types of compensation appear in the literature which we may refer to as supplemental and reactive compensation. In supplemental compensation, *desirable* experiences, behavior, psychological states (for example, autonomy, self-expression, status) that are insufficiently present in the work situation are pursued in a nonwork context. In reactive compensation, *undesirable* work experiences are redressed in a nonwork setting. Examples would include "letting off steam" in response to job tension, resting from fatiguing work; in a word, all forms of *re-creation*. Although supplemental compensation refers to desirable or positive components of works and reactive compensation to undesirable or negative components, underlying both is a common process: deprivations experienced in work are made up or compensated for in nonwork activities.

Spillover hypotheses are equally common. For example, jobs requiring constant disciplined activity may lead some workers to compulsive leisure patterns of being "busy-occupied" and "passing time" since "attitudes acquired during work become so deeply ingrained that they are often carried into the life off the job" (Blum, 1953: 101). In an explicit formulation, Katz (1965: 295) observes that "work habits and interests of the white-collar worker spill over into his family and community life," while Gerstl (1961) has shown that, for some occupations, the presence of specific occupational skills and interests influence the choice of leisure pursuits.

Thus spillover[2] occurs when styles of behavior or of psychological functioning suitable for, or acquired in, the performance of work are transferred to a nonwork context.

Despite their wide use and strong appeal, with few exceptions, writers have applied compensatory and spillover hypotheses speculatively and ad hoc; there has been little systematic effort to specify the conditions under which compensation or spillover is likely to occur, or to explicate the underlying mechanisms involved.

The compensatory and spillover mechanisms are not mutually exclusive, and both may operate at the same time for the same individual. For example, managers and blue-collar workers who both experience their work as insufficiently creative may seek compensation in leisure pursuits. But the manager may compensate by writing, whereas the blue-collar worker might seek creative outlets requiring the use of tools. But the fact that compensation and spillover are alternative modes of explanation has some potentially serious pitfalls. For unless one can specify the conditions under which compensation or spillover are likely to occur, one or the other hypothesis may be used to explain any relationship between work and nonwork. For example, if we find isolation at work associated with solitary leisure patterns this can be explained as resulting from a style of work behavior spilling over into nonwork settings. If, on the other hand, we find isolation at work associated with a high degree of sociability in leisure, this can be accounted for by compensation. Clearly, a theory which permits anything to be explained after the fact is completely lacking in predictive power. The situation is further complicated by the possibility that some workers may respond to a work situation by compensating whereas for other workers the identical situation might produce an opposite spillover response. Thus, while dull, repetitive jobs may lead some workers to compensate by seeking stimulating or creative nonwork alternatives, for others the same job might produce habits of passive mindlessness that would reflect in their leisure. Where such dual patterns occurred in nearly equal proportions there would be no discernible effect of work on nonwork.

Difficulties such as these, resulting from the overlap and potential contradictions, can be resolved only by theoretically specifying the precise conditions under which compensation or spillover is likely, or by utilizing research techniques that discriminate between instances of spillover and those of compensation. Although the former requires a more adequate theory than is now available, relatively straightforward research procedures for detecting spillover and compensation are presently available and will be discussed later in the paper.

As a first step in developing a theory of the effect of work on nonwork, the next section presents a model or paradigm of the work/nonwork relationship that we believe may clarify a number of problems associated with the compensatory and spillover hypotheses.

A PARADIGM FOR THE STUDY OF WORK AND LEISURE

Our review of past research in the sociology of work and leisure indicates two major failures. In the first place, the relationship between work and nonwork activities has not been clearly isolated from the influence of other related variables such as education, class, occupational status, age, and sex. Thus, the relationship between work and nonwork has been confounded. Second, no systematic distinction has been made between the influence of the *structure* of work and that of the *meaning,* or subjective experience, of work upon leisure. We feel that, because of these two failures, sociologists have not been able to specify whether, in any given situation, leisure activity will compensate for, or spill over from, the work experience. In order to generate testable compensatory or spillover hypotheses, we must clearly conceive the complex set of relationships within which work influences nonwork. A model which attempts to do that must separate the effect of work from other

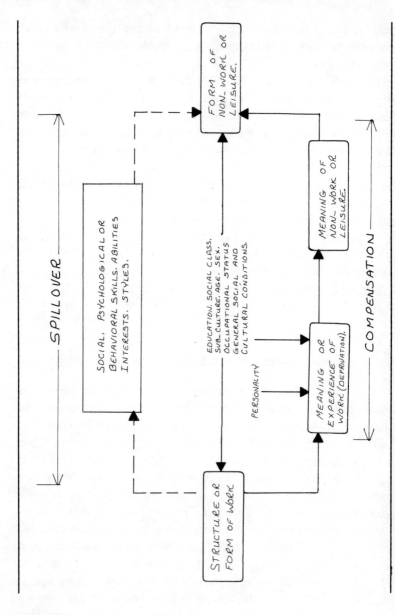

Figure 1: THE RELATIONSHIP BETWEEN WORK AND LEISURE AND OTHER VARIABLES.

variables, distinguish among form and meaning of work and nonwork, and thus demarcate the operation of the compensatory and spillover processes. Figure 1 presents a model which attempts to do this.

Figure 1 indicates how the structure of work—the independent variable—affects leisure patterns—the dependent variable. Essentially, the paradigm suggests two paths by which work affects nonwork: (1) work leads to the development of certain psychological, social, and behavioral skills and life styles which may spill over into nonwork and shape the leisure form; and (2) work, when it leads to a certain subjective experience of deprivation, may result in efforts to compensate for this in nonwork activity.

The mechanism operating in the first of these two paths—the spillover path—is one whereby form (of work) affects form (of nonwork). The mechanism operating in the compensatory path is one whereby meaning (of work) affects meaning and, secondarily, form (of nonwork).

Thus, first, this model indicates the importance of distinguishing between form and meaning: in formulating hypotheses about the relationship between work and nonwork, one must specify whether the hypothesized relationship is one between forms of work and nonwork or between the meanings of work and nonwork. Since the compensatory relationship between the meanings of work and nonwork is at least as important as the spillover relationship between forms of work and nonwork, a one-to-one relationship between specific work forms and nonwork forms can seldom be expected.

In addition, work and nonwork are also affected by social, economic, and cultural variables; personality variables, by influencing the importance of various aspects of work, also affect the meaning of work. Hence, and second, the model indicates a further necessary distinction: the influence of these confounding variables must be isolated from the relationship between work and nonwork. These confounding influences further reduce the probability of one-to-one relationships between specific forms of work and nonwork.

POSSIBLE THEORETICAL DIMENSIONS

OBJECTIVE STRUCTURE OF WORK SITUATION	UNDERLYING MEANING OR SIGNIFICANCE	FORM OR PATTERN OF NON-WORK OR LEISURE
COMPLEXITY SUPERVISION TRAINING SOCIAL CONTACTS TECHNOLOGY ETC.	ALIENATION BOREDOM INTRINSIC EXTRINSIC SELF-ESTEEM INTERESTS SELF-ACTUALIZATION ETC.	SPORTS T.V. VIEWING POLITICAL ACTIVITY ACTIVE-PASSIVE ORDERED-DISORDERED HI BROW-LOW BROW ETC.

POSSIBLE COMBINATIONS

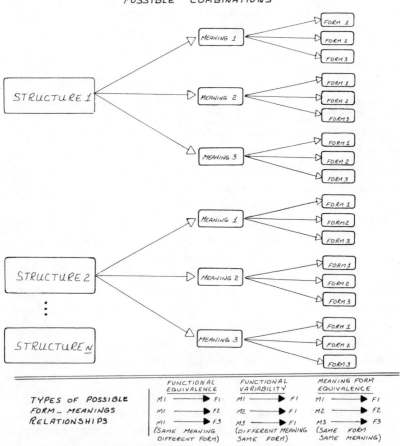

Figure 2: RELATIONSHIP BETWEEN THE STRUCTURE OF WORK, THE FORM OF LEISURE AND THEIR UNDERLYING MEANINGS.

Let us now go back to the theoretical issue of the confusion between form and meaning and the compensatory relationship between work and nonwork. The compensatory mechanism is basically one whereby meaning (of work) affects meaning (of nonwork).

Figure 2 is a schematic representation of the possible ramifications of the dimensions of the work situation into subjective meanings and leisure forms. This model indicates that work and nonwork both have a number of specifiable characteristics. Furthermore, they can both be analyzed in terms of a common and limited set of underlying dimensions of meaning. Beginning with the work situation, it can be hypothesized that any particular characteristic of the work situation (S_1, S_2, S_n) may have a number of possible meanings (M_1, M_2, M_3). In turn, any one of these meanings may lead a person, through compensation, to a number of nonwork forms (F_1, F_2, F_3).

One possibility, then, is that several leisure activites may perform the same compensatory functions for individuals ($M_1 \rightarrow F_1$, $M_1 \rightarrow F_2$, $M_1 \rightarrow F_3$). For example, individuals who spend much of their work time in face-to-face interaction—such as service personnel, waiters, salesmen, barbers—may compensate for this by spending much of their leisure time in nonsocial TV-watching, reading, or individual outdoor activities. The leisure patterns of such individuals may differ depending on social class, age, subculture, and so forth, but they are functionally equivalent in terms of compensation.

On the other hand, the same leisure activity may be engaged in by individuals who experience their work differently ($M_1 \rightarrow F_1$, $M_2 \rightarrow F_1$, $M_3 \rightarrow F_1$). For example, both the advertising agent and the assembly-line worker may frequent a local tavern, the former to compensate for the pressures of his occupation, the latter for the lack of sociability on the job. Thus, the same leisure activity may be compensatory in different ways to different individuals depending on their work experience.

Finally, a given leisure activity may be correlated with a given job experience ($M_1 \rightarrow F_1$, $M_2 \rightarrow F_2$, $M_3 \rightarrow F_3$). For example, individuals who are socially isolated on the job may compensate for this by joining voluntary organizations.

Only this last type of hypothesis seems to have been recognized in past research. Considering the complexity of the possible relationships between the meaning of work and the forms of nonwork, this hypothesis is only one of several alternatives: compensation may not always necessarily be found in the same leisure activity; it may be found in different areas (functional equivalence). A given nonwork form may have been produced by alternative meanings of the work situation (functional variation). And, finally, the nonwork form may be strongly influenced by other variables, including spillover. Whether or not the hypothesis—stating a relationship between a given work form and a given nonwork form—holds, there are serious problems of data interpretation. If it holds, alternative possibilities still have not been eliminated. If it does not hold, there are no grounds to assume that compensation has not occurred in some alternative form of nonwork. Furthermore, the researcher may be tempted to assume, ad hoc, that spillover has occurred (for example, lack of participation in voluntary organizations tends to be interpreted as resulting from the incapacity to engage in meaningful social relations). Without some theoretical or methodological way of specifying logically the conditions under which compensation and spillover occur, or whether functional equivalence and functional variation occur, the compensatory and spillover hypotheses lack all explanatory power.

Future research should be directed toward developing such a theoretical framework or the methodological tools for making such specifications.

FUTURE RESEARCH

It scarcely needs to be pointed out that developing a complete theory of the effect of work upon leisure—one which begins to specify the relationships among the many variables indicated in Figure 1—will be a formidable undertaking, since it will require integrating ideas from a number of diverse subfields, as well as extensive refinements in existing theory. Nevertheless, we believe that the paradigm provides a plausible, if sketchy, outline of the interrelations among the chief elements of such a theory and suggests some relatively fruitful strategies for developing it further while avoiding the confounding effects of other variables, and the confusion between form and meaning.

As a first step, we believe that careful testing of the compensatory hypothesis would prove to be one of the best points to begin testing the theory. Figure 1 shows that the relation between the meaning of work and meaning of leisure, which is the heart of the compensatory hypothesis, may be least affected by confounding variables, or, as we shall later suggest, that the effects of such variables may be easily controlled methodologically. Thus, by focusing initially only upon the relationship between the meaning of work and the meaning of leisure, one need not be concerned with the potentially much more complex relationships among the forms and meanings of work and leisure, or with the possibility of confusing meaning and form.

We believe it should be possible to test the compensatory hypotheses and avoid the variability of work and leisure forms by mapping the diverse forms onto a common set of underlying dimensions of meaning. Efforts should be directed toward a long-needed synthesis of the largely unrelated literature referred to earlier in the paper (note 1) dealing with the meaning of work and the meaning of leisure. The aim should be to derive important dimensions of common meaning underlying work and leisure—for example, their significance for self-esteem, self-actualization, tension-tension release, boredom-excitement, and so forth. By asking respondents parallel sets of questions about their work and leisure behavior that have been framed in terms of such dimensions of meaning it would be possible to establish

(a) the extent to which work is experienced in terms of these dimensions;

(b) the importance of the dimensions;

(c) the extent to which the experiences are felt to be deprivations;

(d) the extent to which leisure is experienced in terms of these dimensions;

(e) the relative importance of the leisure activities.

The relative *importance* of various meaning dimensions will be affected by many variables such as personality characteristics, education, cultural values, and so forth, and the structure of work will largely determine the dimensions in terms of which it is experienced. The advantage of this technique is that by asking respondents about the meaning of work, the complex *causes* behind it are in effect held constant.

If work does affect leisure through supplemental or reactive compensation, we should find that, regardless of what their work may be, individuals who experience it as sufficiently depriving with respect to some dimension will engage in leisure practices to supplement or offset the deprivation on this dimension. Thus, individuals who experience work as isolating and dislike the isolation should also indicate that they engage in one or more leisure pursuits that they experience as sources of sociability.

Determining, by such a technique, whether (or to what extent) compensation occurs would provide a firm theoretical and empirical base for investigating other relationships in the model: the spillover mechanism; the effect of the structure of work on the meaning of work; and the effect of such variables as age, ethnicity, subculture, and values on the forms of leisure.

This paper has attempted to explicate the relationship between work and leisure by addressing itself to the confounding of work with other variables, the confusion between the form of work and leisure and the meaning of work and leisure, and the difficulties in applying the compensation and spillover hypotheses. The paradigm presented here offers one possible way of dealing with these issues.

NOTES

1. There is a vast literature relevant to the meaning of work. It ranges, for example, from the extensive alienation literature flowing from Marx (for example,

Fromm, 1968; Mills, 1956; Blauner, 1964) to surveys of the meaning of work (see Morse and Weiss, 1955; Dubin, 1963; Gurin et al., 1960; Blauner, 1960; Inkeles, 1960; Tausky, 1969), to the psychological literature on job satisfaction (Herzberg et al., 1957; Herzberg, 1966) and studies of the effect of work on mental health (see Kornhauser, 1965; Argyris, 1964). The literature on the meaning of leisure is also diverse. It includes discussions of the cultural meanings of certain sports (Kahn, 1957), the social-psychological meaning of outdoor recreation (Stone, 1955; Stone and Taves, 1956), and the meaning of sociability, art, and travel (Kaplan, 1960a), the psychology of play (Piaget, 1958), games (Goffman, 1961), and the meaning of play in history (Huizinga, 1949). The social and psychological functions of modern mass leisure have been praised (White, 1957; McLuhan, 1965) and criticized (Howe, 1948; Rosenberg, 1957; Boorstin, 1961). Discussions have dealt with its normative meaning (Berger, 1962), its diverse meanings for various groups (Havighurst, 1957), and the proper role and meaning of leisure (DeGrazia, 1962).

2. Two recent articles (Seeman, 1967; Hagedorn and Labovitz, 1968) have referred to this process as *generalization* rather than spillover. We prefer the descriptive if somewhat inelegant term spillover to generalization, however, since it avoids the implication that behavioral or psychological traits acquired in work will be applied *generally* to many leisure activities rather than specifically to a few, an issue which is still problematic.

REFERENCES

Argyris, Chris
    1964 Integrating the Individual and the Organization. New York: John Wiley.
Berger, Bennett M.
    1962 "The sociology of leisure: some suggestions." Industrial Relations 1 (February): 31-45.
Blauner, Robert
    1960 "Work satisfaction and industrial trends in modern society." Pp. 339-360 in W. Galenson and S. M. Lipset (eds.) Labor and Trade Unionism. New York: Free Press.
    1964 Alienation and Freedom: The Factory Worker and His Industry. Chicago: Univ. of Chicago Press.
Blum, Fred H.
    1953 Toward a Democratic Work Process. New York: Harper.
Boorstin, Daniel J.
    1961 The Image: A Guide to Pseudo-Events in America. New York: Harper & Row.
Clarke, Alfred C.
    1956 "Leisure and occupational prestige." Amer. Soc. Rev. 21 (June): 301-307.
DeGrazia, Sebastian
    1962 Of Time, Work and Leisure. Garden City, N.Y.: Doubleday.

Dubin, Robert
1963 "Industrial workers' worlds: a study of the 'central life interests' of industrial workers." Pp. 53-72 in E. O. Smigel (ed.) Work and Leisure: A Contemporary Social Problem. New Haven, Conn.: College and University Press.

Faunce, William A.
1959 "Automation and leisure." Pp. 279-309 in H. Jacobson and J. Roucek (eds.) Automation and Society. New York: Philosophical Library.

Frazier, Edward F.
1957 Black Bourgeoisie. Glencoe, Ill.: Free Press.

Friedmann, Eugene A. and Robert J. Havighurst
1954 The Meaning of Work and Retirement. Chicago: Univ. of Chicago Press.

Fromm, Erich
1968 The Revolution of Hope: Toward a Humanized Technology. New York: Bantam.

Gerstl, Joel E.
1961 "Leisure, taste and occupational milieu." Social Problems 9 (Summer): 56-69.

Goffman, Erving
1961 Encounters. Indianapolis: Bobbs-Merrill.

Gordon, Milton and Charles Anderson
1964 "The blue collar worker at leisure." Pp. 407-416 in A. Shostak and W. Gomberg (eds.) Blue Collar World: Studies of the American Worker. Englewood Cliffs, N.J.: Prentice-Hall.

Gurin, Gerald, Joseph Veroff, and Sheila Feld
1960 Americans View Their Mental Health. New York: Basic Books.

Hagedorn, Robert and Sanford Labovitz
1968 "Participation in community associations by occupation: a test of three theories." Amer. Soc. Rev. 33 (April): 272-283.

Havighurst, Robert J.
1957 "The leisure activities of the middle-aged." Amer. J. of Sociology 53 (September): 152-162.
1960 "Life beyond family and work." Pp. 299-353 in E. W. Burgess (ed.) Aging in Western Societies. Chicago: Univ. of Chicago Press.

Herzberg, Frederick
1966 Work and the Nature of Man. Cleveland: World.
——— B. Mausner, R. Peterson, and D. Capwell
1957 Job Attitudes: Review of Research and Opinions. Pittsburgh: Psychological Services.

Howe, I.
1948 "Notes on mass culture." Politics 5 (Spring): 120-123.

Huizinga, Johan
1949 Homo Ludens: A Study of the Play Elements in Culture. London: Routledge & Kegan Paul.

Inkeles, Alex
    1960 "Industrial man: the relation of status to experience, perception, and value." Amer. J. of Sociology 66 (July): 1-31.
Kahn, Roger
    1957 "Money, muscles, and myths." Nation 185 (July 6): 9-11.
Kaplan, Max
    1960a Leisure in America. New York: John Wiley.
    1960b "The uses of leisure." Pp. 407-443 in C. Tibbits (ed.) Handbook of Social Gerontology: Societal Aspects of Aging. Chicago: Univ. of Chicago Press.
Katz, Fred E.
    1965 "Explaining informal work groups in complex organizations: the case for autonomy in structure." Administrative Sci. Q. 10 (September): 204-223.
Kerr, Clark, J. T. Dunlop, F. H. Harbison, and C. A. Meyers
    1960 Industrialism and Industrial Man. Cambridge, Mass.: Harvard Univ. Press.
Kornhauser, Arthur
    1965 Mental Health of the Industrial Worker. New York: John Wiley.
Kornhauser, William
    1959 The Politics of Mass Society. New York: Free Press.
Lipset, Seymour M.
    1961-1962 "Trade unions and social structure." Industrial Relations 1 (October, February): 75-89, 89-110.
McLuhan, Marshall
    1965 Understanding Media: The Extension of Man. New York: McGraw-Hill.
Mills, C. Wright
    1956 White Collar. New York: Galaxy.
Morse, Nancy C. and Robert Weiss
    1955 "The function and meaning of work." Amer. Soc. Rev. 20 (April): 191-198.
Myrdal, Gunnar
    1944 An American Dilemma. New York: Harper & Row.
Piaget, Jean
    1958 "Criteria of play." Pp. 69-72 in E. Larrabee and R. Meyersohn (eds.) Mass Leisure. Glencoe, Ill.: Free Press.
Reissman, Leonard
    1954 "Class, leisure and social participation." Amer. Soc. Rev. 19 (February): 75-84.
Riesman, David
    1958 "Leisure and work in post-industrial society." Pp. 363-385 in E. Larrabee and R. Meyersohn (eds.) Mass Leisure. Glencoe, Ill.: Free Press.
Rosenberg, Bernard
    1957 "Mass culture in America." Pp. 3-12 in B. Rosenberg and D.

M. White (eds.) Mass Culture: The Popular Arts in America. New York: Free Press.

Seeman, Melvin
1967 "On the personal consequences of alienation in work." Amer. Soc. Rev. 32 (April): 273-285.

Stone, Gregory P.
1955 "American sports: play and display." Chicago Rev. 9 (Fall): 83-100.

——— and M. J. Taves
1956 "Research into the human element in wilderness use." Proceedings of the Society of American Foresters: 26-32.

Tausky, Curt
1969 "Meanings of work among blue collar men." Pacific Soc. Rev. 12 (Spring): 49-54.

Veblen, Thorsten
1899 The Theory of the Leisure Class. New York: Macmillan.

Weber, Max
1958 The Protestant Ethic and the Spirit of Capitalism. New York: Charles Scribner's.

White, David M.
1957 "Mass culture in America: another point of view." Pp. 13-21 in B. Rosenberg and D. M. White (eds.) Mass Culture: The Popular Arts in America. New York: Free Press.

Wilensky, Harold L.
1960 "Work, careers and social integration." International Social Sci. J. 12 (Fall): 543-560.
1964 "Mass society and mass culture: interdependence or independence." Amer. Soc. Rev. 29 (April): 173-197.

CONSEQUENCES OF PARTICIPATION
IN INTERSCHOLASTIC SPORTS

A Review and Prospectus

JOHN C. PHILLIPS
WALTER E. SCHAFER
University of Oregon

Very **few sociological studies** on the role of athletics in high schools appear to have been done prior to 1960. Since that time, a considerable amount of work has appeared, with generally consistent findings on certain aspects of high school athletics. The research the authors are presently doing involves an effort to explain one of those consistent findings—the fact that athletes tend to exceed comparable nonathletes in their achievement of educational goals. In this paper, we will review the evidence on the academic achievement of high school athletes, discuss our efforts to employ the concept of subculture to explain the advantage that athletes enjoy and, finally, speculate on possible broader applications of the kind of work we have been doing.

ATHLETES AND ACADEMIC ACHIEVEMENT

As information about high school athletes has grown more and more plentiful, a number of popular myths about the effects of athletic participation have been supplanted. Perhaps the best example of factual information replacing myth is the relationship between athletic participation and high school scholastic achievement. Athletics has been considered an anti-intellectual influence by some authors (Henry, 1963; Coleman, 1960, 1961, 1966), but there is compelling evidence that athletes get slightly better grades than do comparable non-athletes. Schafer and Armer (1968) found that high school athletes got slightly better grades than nonathletes in their matched sample. Athletes from blue-collar homes and boys who were not in a college-preparatory program got even better grades than their nonathlete counterparts. Bend (1968) found substantially the same pattern. Athletes got slightly better grades and the advantage of athletes was most pronounced among "low-endowment" (low-IQ, low-SES) boys.

The fact that "low-endowment" athletes showed the most pronounced difference in achievement could be important to our interest in subculture as an explanation of these differences. Could it be that athletes are put under special pressure to perform well in the classroom? Perhaps the low-endowment athletes do better than low-endowment nonathletes because they experience pro-educational influences similar to those experienced by middle-class boys.

There is strong evidence to indicate that athletes aspire to and succeed in attending college more than do nonathletes. Bend found that 81.8% of his sample of superior athletes compared to 56.1% of the nonathletes aspired to at least some college education. The figures for low-endowment superior athletes and nonathletes was 39.8% and 13.3% respectively. Over 71% of the superior athletes actually attended college, while 50.0% of the nonathletes attended. Figures for low-endowment athletes and nonathletes were 14.8% and 6.9%. Bend's large sample, longitudinal design, and the fact that the relationship between athletic participation and educational achievement increased as degree of athletic involvement increased inspire confidence in his results. Rehberg and Schafer (1968) and Schafer and Rehberg (1970a, 1970b) found similar patterns in aspirations and expectations for college attendance.

Again, we see blue-collar athletes far exceeding comparable nonathletes in aspirations for college attendance and in the achievement of college attendance. We contend that this difference can be attributed, at least in part, to their experiences as athletes.

Schafer (1969) provides data that indicate that athletes are less likely to be deviant than comparable nonathletes. Again, blue-collar athletes were markedly less likely to be delinquent than blue-collar nonathletes, while the relationship is virtually eliminated among white-collar boys. Schafer argues that, unless some selection factor is working, there must be some influences in athletics that deter boys from engaging in delinquent behavior. We will argue that if potentially delinquent boys were being selected out of athletic participation, then white-collar as well as blue-collar delinquents would be selected. Thus, the negative relationship between athletic participation and delinquency would hold for boys from all socioeconomic backgrounds, not just for lower blue-collar boys.

With the association between athletic participation and educational success especially marked among blue-collar boys, one has firm grounds for expecting more upward social mobility among athletes than among comparable nonathletes. Schafer and Stehr (1968) suggest that, since blue-collar and white-collar athletes are more likely than are nonathletes to associate with the white-collar, college-bound "leading crowd" in high schools (Coleman, 1961: 35-50, 145-151), their mobility chances are enhanced. In a later paper, Schafer and Rehberg (1970a) found that athletes, compared with nonathletes, are more likely to report having been encouraged by teachers and counselors to go on to college. This relationship grows stronger as aspirations for going on to college diminish. Thus it appears that athletes not only attain higher educational achievement, but those who are not disposed toward furthering their education receive special encouragement or sponsorship to do so.

Phillips' (1965) study of college athletes has suggested another possible source of upward mobility among athletes. Phillips found that athletes tended to interact with one another much more than did nonathletes. He argued that this high interaction reduced what Hodges (1964) has termed "the psychic cost of mobility." By having a ready circle of middle-class friends, a blue-collar athlete might better develop the manners, mannerisms, attitudes, and social contacts that facilitate upward mobility. This tendency for athletes to choose other athletes as friends has also been found by Schafer and Rehberg (1970b).

Schafer and Rehberg (1970b: 12) also found that athletes "tend to have close friends who are more positive in educational attitudes, aspirations, and behavior than the close friends of non-athletes." While the nature of their data prohibits firm conclusions, they do suggest the possibility that the differences between athletes and nonathletes can, at least in part, be attributed to their greater exposure to pro-educational peer influences.

We may summarize the evidence on differences between high school athletes and nonathletes as follows:

(1) Athletes generally receive slightly better grades and are more likely to aspire to and attain more education than comparable non-athletes. This is especially marked among athletes from blue-collar homes.

(2) There is some evidence to indicate that athletes are less likely than nonathletes to become delinquent. We do not know whether this relationship is due to selection factors or due to some deterrent effect of athletic participation.

(3) Athletes from blue-collar backgrounds are more likely to be upwardly mobile than nonathletes. This can be explained to a great extent by their greater educational attainment, but other factors such as sponsorship and association may also bear on this mobility.

What are the sources of these differences? Schafer and Armer (1968) suggest several possible explanations. First, athletes may receive special assistance in academic matters from teachers, peers, or coaches. Athletes might simply be graded more leniently. Second, there may be certain organizational requirements that might motivate athletes to perform better than nonathletes. Most high schools require a minimum grade-point average for participation. Athletes may work not only to achieve good enough grades for participation, but to qualify for entry into a college to continue their athletic careers. Third, athletes may be favored by "spillover" of certain qualities they have developed through sport. Higher peer status due to the generalization of their athletic status to other areas of social participation may enhance the athletes' self-esteem and, hence, their motivation to succeed in school work. Values of hard work, excellence, and persistence may be developed in sports activities and applied to academic and other activities. Practice and training regimens may influence athletes to use their study time more efficiently. Fourth, it is possible that conforming, ambitious, able boys tend to go out for sports more than do boys who are less "in tune" with the expectations of the school authorities. That is, athletics selects good students and tends to reject bad students (Schafer, 1969).

One recent article has examined the several possible sources of the educational advantages of athletes. Jerome and Phillips (1971) note the evidence of greater attainment of educational goals by athletes in American high schools. They point out the fact that sports programs in American and Canadian high schools are very similar, but that in Canada athletic partici-pation does not receive the same status and esteem it does in American high schools. The authors argue that if good students, more than poor students, tend to go out for and be selected for athletic teams, the educational advantages of American athletes should exist among Canadian athletes as well. Likewise, if values and habits developed in athletics are applied to one's studies, the Canadian athletes should enjoy the same educational advantages that the American athletes enjoy.

Since the Canadian athletes do not appear to be better than their nonparticipating classmates in the achievement of educa-tional objectives, Jerome and Phillips argue that the source of the American athletes' greater achievement lies not in "spill-over" or selection but in one or more of the other explanations suggested by Schafer and Armer. These explanations (see above) center on *special experiences that are encountered by athletes* but not by nonathletes.

THE ATHLETIC SUBCULTURE

The evidence that athletes in American high schools appear to have certain special experiences, coupled with evidence of differences of behavior between athletes and nonathletes, has led us to the concept of subculture as a possible explanation of the processes intervening between athletic participation and various behavioral outcomes.

We should note here that two of the crucial conditions for the emergence of a subculture exist among athletes—special experiences and high rates of interaction (Phillips and Schafer, 1970). According to Cohen (1955) and Cohen and Short (1958), persons in like circumstances sharing like experiences should tend to develop values, norms, and beliefs (i.e., a subculture) favorable to those in the special circumstances. Our findings indicate that athletes, who experience special rewards in school, tend to develop a pro-school subculture (Phillips and Schafer, 1970).

In two recent papers, Phillips and Schafer (1971, 1970) have tried to develop a conceptual and methodological approach to the study of subcultures. We follow the thinking of Vander Zanden (1970) in conceiving of subculture as values, beliefs, symbols, and norms that are shared among some people but not by the general population. Thus, a subculture exists to the extent that a number of people differ in the norms, values, beliefs, and symbols that they share.

Wolfgang and Ferracuti (1967) point out the problems in measuring the elements of subcultures and point to the salient importance of measuring norms of conduct if we are to study subcultures at all. We contend that, since culture tends "to form a consistent and integrated whole" (Vander Zanden, 1970: 35), we can gain an understanding of all the elements of a subculture by studying any single element—in this case, norms. The return portential model for the measurement of norms (Jackson, 1966, 1960) appears to provide a solution to many of the problems that Wolfgang and Ferracuti cite as impediments to the study of subcultures.

Our recent investigations have been concerned with determining the extent to which there exists a distinguishable subculture shared by interscholastic athletes, and the extent to which such a subculture might account for the differences between athletes and nonathletes reported earlier in this paper.

In a preliminary study of one high school, we found that athletes interact with other athletes much more than do nonathletes, and, while athletes appear to expect the same kinds of conduct from their friends, the norms shared by the athletes are much more intense and more likely to regulate behavior. That is, athletes appear to be under greater pressure to conform to conventional school standards than are nonathletes (Phillips and Schafer, 1970). This greater pressure to conform to conventional standards of behavior is reflected from time to time in newspaper stories depicting often sharp controversies regarding the misbehavior of athletes (albeit not high school athletes). Few college students need fear reprisals for wearing beards or mustaches, but one can read about athletes being removed from their team rosters for even so minor a transgression.

We are also interested in the role of the coach as a link between the official school culture and the athletic subculture, which, as we have discussed above, reflects the official school culture. We believe that coaches affect not only the norms shared among athletes but the individual athletes themselves. To the extent that we find the official school norms, values, and beliefs being transmitted through the coach to the athletes, and the norms, values and beliefs they share, we will be able to explain the tendency of athletes to conform to the official school goals of academic achievement and conventional conduct.

While we have emphasized the positive outcomes of interscholastic athletics, we are interested in some of the criticisms of highly competitive interscholastic athletics as well. Could it be that the more conventional athletes tend toward intergroup and interpersonal intolerance, uncritical acceptance of existing systems, and a disinterest in public affairs? Since they are rewarded by the "system," athletes may well resist change and reform. We know of one recent incident where high school athletes joined together to suppress an effort by certain other students to challenge a number of school rules.

FURTHER RESEARCH

Until now, we have discussed only the possible existence of subcultural influences on American high school athletes and how those influences might produce the differences we have observed between athletes and nonathletes. We have paid little attention to collegiate athletes, club athletes, and professional athletes. Neither have we sought to investigate the possible impact of the game itself on the participant. These questions promise to be interesting and important if the existing literature is any indication. Weinberg and Arond (1952), Charnofsky (1968), and Scott (1968) respectively provide us with insights on the occupational culture of boxers, baseball players, and jockeys. They discuss the role of superstitions, norms regarding physical courage, beliefs about how one might best win, the athletes' image of themselves, and other matters that suggest the presence of an occupational subculture and, perhaps, certain shared norms, values, beliefs, and symbols that stem from the participants' common interest in the game, but extend to matters external to sports.

Another focus on subcultures in sport might involve participants' commitment to the official value system of a given sports organization or movement. Hans Lenk (1964) has investigated athletes' commitments to the traditional and official aims and values of the Olympic games. He has also examined the implications of the postwar tendency of German athletes to be committed to their clubs only in the realm of sport, not in other aspects of their lives (Lenk, 1966). We would expect the degree of athletes' commitment to sports organizations to strongly influence the degree to which the official organizational norms regulate the behavior of club athletes.

It is possible that a national sports movement might enhance certain government efforts toward social change. Wohl (1969a, 1969b) discusses how sports clubs have helped to reduce certain traditional hostilities based on social and geographical origins, as well as replacing certain backward peasant traditions with more open, modern modes of behavior. We would hope to someday examine the condition of peasant and worker sports club participants and nonparticipants to determine if patterns exist that are similar to those we have observed in American high school athletes.

A final aspect of sports that might play a role in the generation of subcultural influences is the meaning of the game to the participants. Webb (1969) discusses the way in which attitudes toward sport are "professionalized." While young children tend to just play at their games, older children appear to place an increasing emphasis on skill and winning. Heinila (1969) employs a similar notion of playing for the sake of a "good match" and playing to win. Whether a team emphasizes the game (good match) or the game outcome (winning), may determine the nature of the interpersonal and organizational relationships among members of the team. These relationships may, in turn, influence the development of subculture among the participants.

In summary, we have convincing evidence that American interscholastic athletes achieve educational goals more than do comparable nonathletes. We have some preliminary evidence that indicates that the athletes share norms that exert a strong pro-school influence on them, and that these norms appear to fit our concept of subculture. We are still investigating the sources and content of this apparent athletic subculture. In the future, we hope to investigate whether subcultures develop among athletes in certain sports, or among members of sports clubs or organizations. We also hope to employ the concepts of professionalization of and commitment to sports and determine their impact, if any, on the development of subcultures in sport. If athletes collectively or individually continue to exert the influence they have in the recent past, the nature of any athletic subculture could take on an increasing importance that extends beyond the world of sport.

REFERENCES

Bend, Emil
 1968 The Impact of Athletic Participation on Academic and Career Aspiration and Achievement. New Brunswick, N.J.: National Football Foundation and Hall of Fame.

Charnofsky, Harold
  1968 "The major league professional baseball player: self-conception versus the popular image." International Rev. of Sport Sociology 3: 39-55.
Cohen, Albert K.
  1955 Delinquent Boys: The Culture of the Gang. Glencoe, Ill.: Free Press.
– – – and James F. Short, Jr.
  1958 "Research in delinquent subcultures." J. of Social Issues 14: 20-37.
Coleman, James S.
  1960 "Adolescent subculture and academic achievement." Amer. J. of Sociology 65 (January): 337-347.
  1961 The Adolescent Society. New York: Free Press.
  1966 "Peer cultures and education in modern society." Pp. 266-269 in T. M. Newcomb and E. K. Wilson (eds.) College Peer Groups: Problems and Prospects for Research. Chicago: Aldine.
Heinila, Kalevi
  1969 "Football at the crossroads." International Rev. of Sport Sociology 4: 5-30.
Henry, Jules
  1963 Culture Against Man. New York: John Wiley.
Hodges, Harold M., Jr.
  1964 Social Stratification: Class in America. Cambridge: Schenkman.
Jackson, Jay
  1960 "Structural characteristics of norms." Pp. 136-163 in The Dynamics of Instructional Groups. Yearbook of the National Society for the Study of Education. Chicago: Univ. of Chicago Press.
  1966 "A conceptual and measurement model for norms and roles." Pacific Soc. Rev. 9 (Spring): 63-72.
Jerome, Wendy C. and John C. Phillips
  1971 "The relationship between academic achievement and inter-scholastic participation: a comparison of Canadian and American high schools." C. A. H. P. E. R. J. 37 (January/February): 18-21.
Lenk, Hans
  1964 Werte, Ziele, Wirklichkeit der Modernen Olympischen Spiele (Values, Aims, Reality of the Modern Olympic Games). Scharndorf bei Stuttgart: Karl Hofmann.
  1966 "Total or partial engagement? Changes regarding personal ties with the sports club." International Rev. of Sport Sociology 1: 85-108.
Phillips, John C.
  1965 "Motivation for participation in athletics: an exploratory study." M.A. thesis. San Jose State College.

— — — and Walter E. Schafer
    1970 "The athletic subculture: a preliminary study." Presented at the annual meetings of the American Sociological Association, Washington, D.C.
    1971 "Subcultures in sport: a conceptual and methodological model." In Publication 2 of the Research Institute of the Swiss Federal School of Gymnastics and Sport. Basel: Birkhauser.
Rchberg, Richard A. and Walter E. Schafer
    1968 "Participation in interscholastic athletics and college expectations." Amer. J. of Sociology 73 (May): 732-740.
Schafer, Walter E.
    1969 "Participation in interscholastic athletics and delinquency: a preliminary study." Social Problems 17 (Summer): 40-47.
— — — and J. Michael Armer
    1968 "Athletes are not inferior students." Trans-action (November): 21-26, 61-62.
Schafer, Walter E. and Richard A. Rehberg
    1970a "Athletic participation, college aspirations, and college encouragement." University of Oregon. (unpublished)
    1970b "Athletic participation, peer influences, and educational aspirations: toward a theory of the athletic subculture." University of Oregon. (unpublished)
Schafer, Walter E. and Nico Stehr
    1968 "Participation in competitive athletics and social mobility, some intervening social processes." Presented at the meetings of the International Committee on Sociology of Sport, Vienna, Austria.
Scott, Marvin B.
    1968 The Racing Game. Chicago: Aldine.
Vander Zanden, James W.
    1970 Sociology. A Systematic Analysis. New York: Ronald Press.
Webb, Harry
    1969 "Professionalization of attitudes toward play among adolescents." Pp. 161-178 in Gerald S. Kenyon (ed.) Aspects of Contemporary Sport Sociology. Chicago: Athletic Institute.
Weinberg, S. Kirson and Henry Arond
    1952 "The occupational culture of the boxer." Amer. J. of Sociology 57 (March): 460-469.
Wohl, Andrzej
    1969a "Integrational functions of sport." In Publication 2 of the Research Institute of the Swiss Federal School of Gymnastics and Sport. Basel: Birkhauser.
    1969b "Engagement in sports activity on the part of the workers of large industrial establishment in peoples Poland." International Rev. of Sport Sociology 4: 83-127.
Wolfgang, Marvin E. and Franco Ferracuti
    1967 The Subculture of Violence. London: Tavistock.

THE WILDLAND RECREATION BOOM AND SOCIOLOGY

WILLIAM R. CATTON, Jr.
University of Canterbury (New Zealand)

The **explosive expansion of wildland recreation** in recent decades merits sociological attention not only because of the important social changes with which it is connected, but because it is in itself a sociologically challenging change in the life styles of various Western societies. Recreation can be viewed as a social institution (National Academy of Sciences, 1969). Its features and functions are as distinctive and sociologically interesting as those of the social structures engaged in economic production, whose study has acquired from the Protestant ethic a more widely recognized legitimacy.

Within an exclusively American context, the writer accepted this frame of reference and studied patterns of travel to national parks (Catton and Berggren, 1964; Catton, 1965), characteristics, values, normative attitudes, and management preferences of wilderness users (Hendee and Catton, 1968; Hendee et al., 1968), and the motivations of wildland recreation (Catton, 1969). On the assumption that the confinement of such studies to the American scene probably imposed unknown limitations upon the insights they afforded, the writer came to feel that it would be sociologically enlightening to acquire some familiarity with similar institutions in a different society. This paper reports new perspectives acquired since the writer has resided in New Zealand.

Cooley (1909) and Mead (1934) showed the importance of play in the socialization process. Huizinga (1950) has argued that the existence of civilization depends upon play elements whereby self-mastery is learned and individuals acquire the capacity and the tendency to commit themselves to conventional rules and to socially agreed concepts of fairness in their interactions. There is no reason to exclude from these conceptions the forms of play that occur in wildland contexts.

Such forms are no longer rare and can no longer be left out of the province of sociology, except arbitrarily. Outdoor recreation management has become a function of the federal government, with more than eighty of its agencies spending hundreds of millions of dollars annually, and requiring guidance from research that is largely still undone. A few figures will suffice to give an idea of the magnitude of this sociologically uncharted sector of human behavior. According to a 1965 sample survey by the U.S. Bureau of Outdoor Recreation, during the summer of that year, Americans participated in 97 million man-days of camping. There were 117 million man-days of participation in nature walks, 50 million man-days of hiking, and even the relatively esoteric sport of mountain climbing occupied 4 million man-days. In some circles, the phrase "bird watcher" remains a derogatory epithet, but there were 17 million man-days devoted to wildlife and bird photography. Unless all of these forms of recreational behavior could be shown to be altogether nonsocial, involving no *interaction* among persons, groups, organizations, and normative systems, they are of sufficient magnitude to provide an important arena for sociological inquiry.

Theoretical analysis of the nature of play leads into topics that have long been accorded legitimacy in sociology even when the study of play was largely disdained. Questions of the nature and origin of religious concepts, for example, can become involved (Huizinga, 1950). Sacred acts typically occur in special, sanctified places. According to Huizinga, this is best explained by noting a play element in the origin of ritual, and then noting that people make a distinction between their play and their work. This distinction is commonly emphasized by the occurrence of play in specially designated locations—playgrounds. Within these areas, special rules apply, creating a special social order. People value that special order, sometimes very strongly. This is indicated by the fact that people impose sanctions at least as severe upon the "spoilsport," who implicitly denies the special order by refusing to play, as upon the "cheat" who merely deviates from the rules in the course of play (Huizinga, 1950). Religious antipathy toward the apostate similarly tends to be more severe than toward the sinner. "Formally speaking, there is no distinction whatever between marking out a space for a sacred purpose and marking it out for purposes of sheer play" (Huizinga, 1950: 20).

NATIONAL PARKS: PLAYGROUND SANCTUARIES

The sociological equivalence of the playground and the ritual site is nowhere better shown than in the movement for wilderness preservation. Impetus for the preservation of wilderness comes partly from a quasi-religious ecological conscience contending that human societies are obliged to provide special opportunities for existing ecosystems of plants and animals to survive in places insulated from human impact. Impetus also comes from the human quest for refreshing and pleasurable escape from the world of work (Darling and Eichhorn, 1967). The creation of national parks has been a major institutional expression of this movement.

Huizinga believed the play element was fundamental in culture-building. It is a reasonable extension of his hypothesis to suggest that normative expectations governing man's relations to his fellow creatures (including other humans) could evolve in the context of recreational visits to nature sanctuaries and could have greater survival value for homo sapiens than systems of norms which have prevailed in less exalted environments (see Klausner, 1969).

National park use is *social* behavior, sociologically researchable. Visits to national parks are overwhelmingly made by *families,* and the use of national park campgrounds is especially a family activity (National Park Service, 1956). Tendencies to spend leisure time in this way, and receptivity to the norms and values implicit in such behavior, vary with socioeconomic status (Hendee et al., 1968). Life-cycle development of wildland recreation preferences seems to resemble "career" development as studied by occupational sociologists. Patterns of "recruitment"of wilderness devotees and choice of recreational activities and habitats may fall into stages of progression from one level of maturity to another, which depend on surmounting barriers—social, psychological, financial, geographic, and physiological (National Academy of Sciences, 1969).

As playgrounds, the national parks have become the locales of behavior patterns that eminently belong to the sociological domain. On Independence Day, 1966, for example, 54,000 visitors congregated in or passed through the Yosemite Valley, scenic heart of Yosemite National Park. Campgrounds were heavily crowded and the incidence of crime was serious. To provide for such crowds, there had developed in the valley nine stores selling groceries and general tourist supplies, seven service stations, three swimming pools, hotels accommodating 4,500 people, a stock stable, a barbershop, and a laundry (Darling and Eichhorn, 1967). The fragility of the special social order created by the rules of play or by concepts of sacredness is plain to see in such places.

On a study tour of national parks in the United States and Canada, the Director of National Parks and Reserves in New Zealand was impressed with the law enforcement problems created even in the parks by increasing rebellion against authority. "Drugs and drunkenness with young people 'doing their thing' saw 105 arrests and 44 people jailed in Yosemite Valley one July weekend and here and in some other parks thefts are common and there are even cases of armed robbery in the parks." In problem areas, park staff have to be equipped with sidearms and even with mace or other crowd-control devices. They must "learn to identify plants used for illicit drug production; some are known to have been planted in the parks for later harvesting." (This is, in Huizinga's terms, a use of the playground or sacred site for a purpose that denies its special status.) "The upshot is that many rangers, entering the Park Service because of their interest in natural resources [that is, in the special qualities of the site] find themselves preoccupied with dealing with problems of rebellious people" (Lucas, 1970: 59).

Calls for sociological attention to human interactions in wildland contexts did not have to await the emergence of such dramatic threats to recreational resource managers' morale. In his presidential message to the Pacific Sociological Society, Glen E. Carlson (1943) described the creation of regional councils on human relations in forestry under the auspices of the American Association for the Advancement of Science, at the request of the U.S. Forest Service. He outlined studies then under way and mentioned other conceivable research contributions to forest management practice and to social science knowledge. But there was a war going on. Problems of the kind discussed here were thus overshadowed by events everyone regarded as "more serious."

ERRORS, TRENDS, AND ECOLOGICAL PROBLEMS

Reduction of the volume of pleasure travel during World War II temporarily eased and postponed the full impact of visitor pressure on the national parks. Little attention was devoted by sociologists and other social scientists to such matters. Coordination of available social science knowledge with ecological insights remained nascent. Neither sufficed to prevent serious damage to the parks when visitation rates exploded after the war. Hindsight suggests that sociology might have helped prevent serious miscalculations and strongly regretted side effects from the remedial measures undertaken by the National Park Service. In 1956, problems of overuse were sufficiently out of hand to extract financial support from the U.S Congress for a ten-year development program called "Mission 66" to be completed by the fiftieth anniversary of the National Park Service. It was intended to "provide the physical facilities . . . to reduce the impact of public use on superlative and often fragile features" of the nation parks.

More sophisticated methods of projecting park visitation rates, assessing their impact, and perhaps even inhibiting people from coming to the parks were needed and might have been provided by sociologists had they recognized the theoretical and applied significance of such problems. The National Park Service itself saw Mission 66 as "an endeavor to look into the future . . . and to plan for it." It described the National Park System (including not only the national parks, but also the national monuments, historical and military parks, parkways, recreation areas, seashores, and capital parks) as having been developed and staffed to serve something like 25 million visitors. In 1956, the annual visitor load was about twice that capacity, and the Service anticipated *80 million visits a year by 1966* (National Park Service, 1956: 10, 12, 14). But, by 1966, the total number of visits to all areas in the system had shot past the anticipated 80 million to a staggering *133 million*. An error of such magnitude by a responsible administrative agency in projecting the volume of any socially meaningful human activity must surely challenge sociologists (a) to discover how the mark could be so badly missed, and (b) to explore the social implications of the unexpected increment. [Since completion of the Mission 66 program, the growth in visitor numbers has continued to accelerate; each year's total has exceeded the previous year's total by an increasing difference! Is this another instance, the sociologist must ask, of the efforts designed to cope with a problem having the unexpected side effect of instigating more of the behavior from which the problem arises? Are there any *general* criteria, he should also wonder, by which problems that tend to evoke counterproductive "remedies" can be recognized?]

With wildland recreation now so much a part of the American way of life, it is easy to forget how much of a change it represents and how recent that change has been. Bearing in mind the huge totals of visitor numbers in the last few years, it is striking to note that in 1916, just before Congress enacted the law to coordinate administration of the parks by a National Park Service, the fourteen areas in the nascent National Park System which estimated or counted visitors reported a year's total of only 358,000.

Ecological preservation of such "tourist attractions"as Yellowstone and Yosemite was relatively feasible when access roads and the nation's highways were poorly developed, when few families owned automobiles, when the work week was long, and paid vacations were rare. Changes in all these variables have had much impact upon wilderness, and this makes the ecology of wild areas distinctly *human* ecology. Conversely, the act of legally classifying certain areas as wilderness is more than a specimen of political behavior; it is, in an important sense, an ecological phenomenon.

Of those who did visit national parks in 1916, 98% came by rail! Today, rail travel to national parks is almost nil. Of equal sociological significance to the displacement of rail travel by the family auto is the residential distribution of potential visitors. In the 1920 census, almost half the U.S. population still fell into the "rural" category. Continued urbanization of the nation has been a major contributing factor in the explosion of visitor volume. As a Conservation Foundation staff member has said, "At Yosemite the tremendous weekend influx of visitors from Los Angeles seeking recreation and entertainment is as much a commentary about the limitations of the environment of Los Angeles as it is about the attractions of Yosemite" (Eddy, 1967). National park problems and urban problems are inextricably entwined.

ECOLOGICAL ETHICS

Sociologists who remain uninterested in "merely" recreational environments such as national parks are likely to remain unaware of bodies of literature having much to offer them. While sociologists were preoccupied with the Great Depression, a conservationist published in a forestry journal an incisive essay on the relevance of ethics and ecology to each other which deserves the attention of sociologists today. Leopold (1933) described civilization not as it is so widely imagined to be, "the enslavement of a stable and constant earth," but as "a state of mutual and interdependent cooperation between human animals, other animals, plants, and soils, which may be disrupted at any moment by the failure of any of them." From this ecological premise, Leopold edged toward sociology. "The conservation movement is," he said (1933: 48), "at the very least, an assertion that these interactions . . . are too important to be left to chance, even that sacred variety of chance known as economic law." And he was on sociological ground, surely, in adding, "We have three possible controls: legislation, self-interest, and ethics." He urged an extension of ethics which would stress man's obligations toward the ecosystems in which he is involved and would supersede the traditional one-way definition of natural resources as "property."

From the perspective of biology, Leopold (1933: 44) observed that an ethic is "a limitation on freedom of action in the struggle for existence." In the more usual framework, an ethic is "a differentiation of social from antisocial conduct." Either way, "The thing has its origins in the tendency of interdependent individuals or societies to evolve modes of cooperation. The biologist calls these symbioses." Political and economic processes are advanced symbioses elaborated by man. The first yardstick for assessing such symbioses was expediency. But as population density increased and as more effective tools were developed, the symbioses grew more complex. Expediency was no longer sufficient as a yardstick, and ethical yardsticks began to be superimposed. Sociologists could envy the felicity of Leopold's (1933: 45) phrasing when he said, "An ethic may be regarded as a mode of guidance for meeting ecological situations so new or intricate, or involving such deferred reactions, that the path of social expediency is not discernible to the average individual."

A PERENNIAL DILEMMA

The wildland recreation explosion has made plainly visible a dilemma that was inherent in the concept of a national park and that represents the sociologically significant problem of a "fallacy of composition." The dilemma is firmly embedded in the National Parks Act of 1916. This act created the National Park Service and required it to "conserve the scenery and the natural and historic objects and the wild life" in the national parks and (failing to see any contradiction) "to provide for the enjoyment of the same in such manner and by such means as will leave them unimpaired for the enjoyment of future generations" (Ise, 1961: 191-192). The Congressional mandate was to foster use and prevent change. Folk knowledge saw nothing illusory in this combination of goals; nor did it foresee how illusory it would become as volume of use reached undreamed-of levels. Folk knowledge on many matters is, according to Boulding (1964), subject to fallacies of composition which it is the task of social science to correct.

Descriptions of collective processes in individual terms, or descriptions of mass action in terms that connote primary group phenomena, seem plausible, but are often seriously misleading. To an individual in certain circumstances, to be strong is to be safe, but when many sovereign nations seek safety in military strength, they become threats to each other. A forest primeval is a place of tranquility, solitude, and inspiration to its visitors—if they remain sufficiently few in number. As their rewarding experience of it increases the frequency of their visits to it, however, it *ceases to be* a forest primeval, and all lose what each sought.

In comparison with national park systems, few institutions offer the sociologist such clear opportunities to investigate factors that impede or facilitate comprehension of fallacies of composition. In such investigations, sociologists may encounter once more the old-fashioned process of compromise. The chairman of Australia's Academy of Science Committee on

National Parks has said of this problem, "A national park without man is without significance to man, but man by his presence alters the attributes we wish to preserve. . . . How to compromise for the greatest good for the largest number and for the longest time is the question to be answered by parks administrators" (Day, 1962: 157). But some sociologists may recognize that the benefits of compromise are limited by the mathematical impossibility of maximizing more than one variable at a time in a partial differential equation. A biologist has suggested that national parks might be sold as private property to limit use, or they might be kept public but with deliberate allocation of rights to enter (Hardin, 1968: 1245):

> The allocation might be on the basis of wealth, by the use of an auction system. It might be on the basis of merit, as defined by some agreed-upon standards. It might be by lottery. Or it might be on a first-come, first-served basis, administered to long queues. These I think, are all the reasonable possibilities. They are all objectionable. But we must choose—or acquiesce in the destruction of the commons that we call our National Parks.

A long-time member of the New Zealand National Parks Authority has suggested that the only way of resolving the dilemma may be to preserve most of a park's area in primeval condition by concentrating visitor facilities and accommodations in a small fraction of it which thus becomes virtually a "rural slum" (McCaskill, 1965). Proceeding from such an assumption, the sociologist may raise the question whether *urban* slums are any less functional as components of an adaptive community structure. Or, conversely, he may suggest that insofar as cities have been able to reduce their slums, the functional alternatives by means of which they have done so could indicate comparable ways of avoiding the slum-concentration method of wildland protection.

DIFFUSION OF AN IDEA

The national park idea has been involved in an important and sociologically illuminating process of cultural diffusion. Not all innovations diffuse so widely or are embraced with such conviction. This one was sired by the eighteenth- and nineteenth-century Romantic Movement, with its emphasis upon nature. The idea was born during exploration of the Yellowstone territory in 1870, when the members of the exploring party were inspired to forswear mercenary exploitation of the wonders they had seen. The idea began to be formally institutionalized in the Yellowstone Park Act of 1872. It has diffused to all parts of the world in the ensuing century.

As various nations have created national parks, they have not always at first seen the full implications of what they were purporting to do. According to a Canadian pamphlet, *Wisdom's Heritage* (1961), distributed by the Canadian park service,

> Establishing a national park means giving up for all time to come the possible economic advantages of exploiting the material resources of the area concerned and receiving in exchange nothing more than those intangible benefits that belong in the realm of the spirit. . . . When Parliament creates national parks, it speaks for the soul of Canada, and not for its pocket-book.

Clearly, this is a fundamental innovation in land use and in the regulation of human behavior.

By implementing this idea so energetically and with a remarkable degree of success, the United States (today so unpopular abroad in certain other respects) "has continued to be an inspiration to the rest of the world . . . the National Park System and the National Park Service of the United States are looked up to in a very special way" (Darling and Eichhorn, 1967: 9). An Amsterdam travel agent, among a group of other travel agents, industrial executives, and embassy officials, who were shown a series of color slides by two American park rangers touring Europe with other government officials and representatives of American travel industries, commented: "You have shown us for the first time that America has a heart." He appreciated learning by this means, he said, that the United States has "kept some places wild and free and dedicated to the highest of ideals" (Sutton, 1965: 137).

The idea has now diffused to more than eighty nations, which have established national parks or equivalent reserves. In 1948, under UNESCO auspices, the International Union for the Conservation of Nature was created. From headquarters in Switzerland, it works to preserve wildlife and landscape, and to foster resource conservation. It has sought to develop an international definition of a national park, partly in response to an alleged tendency of some nations to designate as national parks areas that have too little significance but that might by that title attract unwary American tourists (Lucas, 1970).

New Zealand was one of the first countries to adopt the national park idea after the United States, but according to a New Zealand biologist active in the park protection movement, park legislation in New Zealand has more loopholes which permit incompatible economic development than do the relevant American statutes (Salmon, 1960). Nevertheless, the writer's impression from a year's residence in New Zealand and from observation of public clamor against a scenery-damaging hydroelectric proposal for Fiordland National Park is that the national park idea is as well understood and as firmly rooted in New Zealand public opinion as in American. One can, therefore, question the generality of the anthropological view (Linton, 1936) that, in the diffusion of a cultural element, there is a descending rank order of diffusibility of its form, use, meaning, and function. This needs further study.

New Zealanders in and out of government have been impressively receptive students of the American pattern of park protection, even though Britain, not the United States, remains the principal overseas reference group for New Zealanders in many other matters. A New Zealand couple who had camped their way across North America en route to Britain to continue their studies, wrote to the National Parks Authority in Wellington: "There are a lot of things in the U.S.A. we hope N.Z. never adopts, but we leave America very impressed with their National Park Service" (Lucas, 1970: 84). New Zealand government publications on the subject (for example, *National Parks of New Zealand*) consistently honor the American precedent. The National Parks Authority has explicitly sought to learn from the exemplary efforts of more senior park services overseas and has also been alert to problems it might avoid "as a result of their mistakes rather than our own" (Lucas, 1970: 4).

New Zealand attitudes on these matters are so thoroughly unchauvinistic that, in a world beset with national jealousies and antipathies, they beg explanation. I can only offer at the moment three unconfirmed hypotheses:

(1) that a small, insular, and socially stable nation which can be no threat to its far-flung neighbors feels no jealousy because it provokes none;

(2) that the national park idea has an inherent capacity to appeal to the nobler nature of man in any nation;

(3) that New Zealand's confidence in the soundness of its own national park system is sufficient for it to assume that diffusion of administrative techniques will be a two-way exchange, mutually beneficial.

All three hypotheses have some plausibility in light of the following facts. Canadians, living next door to the American giant sometimes find identity a vexatious problem. The Canadian publication, *Wisdom's Heritage* (1961), was less magnanimous than comparable New Zealand pamphlets and, in its review of seventy years of national park history in Canada, made no mention at all of the Yellowstone precedent, while praising the foresight of Canadians of an earlier generation. The U.S. National Park Service has described New Zealand's national parks as "international in significance"; New Zealand's Director of National Parks and Reserves has said that his country has much to offer as well as much to gain from participation in the IUCN: and a Working Party on National Parks Administration in New Zealand solicited papers from overseas sources, including one from the National Park Service of the United States, for which its report expressed special appreciation.

The lesson for sociology seems to be that, under favorable circumstances that need to be specified by further studies, *cultural diffusion can be quite deliberate, open, solicited by the receiving society, generously given, and genuinely appreciated.* One wonders, upon reflection, when, where, and which religious missionaries may have experienced this, or, for that matter, how many sociologists today are too conflict-oriented to believe it.

IMPORTANCE OF LOW DENSITY

New Zealand's claim to a leadership position among the world's national park systems is supported by data given in Table 1. Even more than in the United States, recency of settlement appears in the light of such data to have been a major circumstance facilitating the "setting aside" of land in New Zealand for national park purposes. Sociologists would do well to keep in mind the strong institution-breeding and culture-shaping potential of sheer population density and other aspects of the relation of mankind to non-man-made environments.

By comparison, not until after World War II did densely populated Britain join the worldwide movement to set up national parks. A number of scenically attractive areas in England and Wales were designated as national parks by a National Parks Commission created by act of Parliament. They embrace roughly nine percent of the area of England and Wales, but more than 250,000 people continue to reside in them and their protection from "incongruous or harmful development . . . is more apparent than real." There have been a number of serious intrusions since their establishment—industrial developments, power stations, defense installations (Gilbert, 1964).

INSTITUTIONAL LIFE CYCLES

Visiting national parks in New Zealand after observing the effects of overuse in the American national parks has given the author the impression of turning back the clock. New Zealand's

TABLE 1
SOME RELEVANT COMPARISONS BETWEEN NEW ZEALAND AND THE UNITED STATES

	New Zealand	United States
Population (1970)	2.8 million	204 million
Territory	103,736 sq.mi.	3,615,211 sq.mi.
Territory per capita		
Total at time first national park was created (N.Z., 1887; U.S., 1872)	106 acres	45 acres
Total at time of enactment of National Parks Act (N.Z., 1952; U.S., 1916)	33 acres	19 acres
Total at present (1970)	23.7 acres	11.3 acres
National park acres per capita (1970)	1.804	0.069
Number of national parks (1970)	10	35
Mean park size	507,000 acres	405,000 acres
Largest national park	3,023,713 acres	2,213,207 acres
Smallest national park	45,134 acres	912 acres
Ratio of national parks to population	1 national park for every 280,000 people	1 national park for every 5,850,000 people
Percentage of nation's territory designated as national parks	7.62% (1 acre in every 13)	0.61% (1 acre in every 164)
Government expenditures per year on national parks (capital development, operations and maintenance) as fraction of GNP (approximate)	$1 of every $10,000	$1 of every $8,000

SOURCES: Ise, 1961; Lucas, 1970; New Zealand Official Yearbook, 1970; Statistical Abstracts of the United States, 1968; newspapers.

national parks seem to recapture now an earlier, happier phase in American national park history. One feels tempted anew by Spenglerian analogies between stages of history and episodes in an individual organism's life cycle. The writer is, of course, entirely in accord with Nisbet's (1969) reasons for rejecting such notions and for deploring the intellectual effects of the growth metaphor generally. Nevertheless, it strikes a responsive chord in the writer when an ecologist and a geographer ask, "Was there a moment of optimum in the history of the National Park System of the United States?" and particularly when they suggest that

. . . 1935-1940 was in the nature of a peak of both achievement and enjoyment. Morale in the service was very high and the visitors found it possible to gain that experience of a national park which had been the ideal of the pioneers of the movement. Architectural standards were high, there was a beginning of ecological awareness within the Park Service, and pressures from visitors and cars were lower [Darling and Eichhorn, 1967: 22].

The apparent recapitulation in New Zealand of this earlier American condition leads one to think sociologists should not too lightly or too dogmatically dismiss the hypothesis of some typical succession of stages in the life cycle of an institution or even of a society. Sociologists could consider that kind of hypothesis empirically, without having to assume that all institutional change is "developmental" or "immanent" (and if thus uncaused, therefore inexplicable). Typical sequences of stages in institutional *evolution* could arise from dependence on environmental circumstances and cumulative processes of adaptation. According to Darling and Eichhorn (1967: 21),

There is, in the histories of communities in relation to their resource base, a period of learning how to reach the resource and use it, followed by a period of rich enjoyment which seems endless in that happy time; then there comes a choice of working out the resource and losing it, or learning the art and science of conservation that the resource may be perpetuated by wise use.

IMPACT OF TECHNOLOGY

Recent sociological discussion of social change has focused too narrowly on deviance, conflict, power, and so forth, and the once exaggerated role of technology is almost eclipsed. Comparison of New Zealand national parks with certain national parks in Canada has reminded the writer that technology can play a central part in shaping sequences of stages in institutional evolution. Three of Canada's large national parks in the Rocky Mountains happen to lie on main transcontinental rail routes. Railway construction somewhat antedated park establishment and far antedated full institutionalization of a preservationist ethic. Hence there developed within Banff, Jasper, and Yoho sizable townsites–functioning first as support centers for railroad-building and operation, serving later as tourist resorts. Recent efforts by Canada's federal government to deurbanize these parks have had little visible effect and have been a discouraging uphill struggle.

In one of New Zealand's long-established national parks, there is a similar, though smaller, railway town. More striking, however, in its reflection of domination by a *newer* technology, is the following faintly fatalistic statement by the Director of National Parks and Reserves: "Public use of aircraft for access and sightseeing is well established in several New Zealand parks; it enables the public to reach remote lakes and sounds and to visit alpine snowfields." But he adds, "It is certainly essential, if a wilderness atmosphere is to be preserved, that visitors to some areas of national parks be free of disturbance from low-flying aircraft" (Lucas, 1970: 15). As park flights grow in number, the future of national park tranquility may be indicated by legal claims already made for loss of property value by homeowners in urban airport flight paths. But there is a lesson for sociologists in the survival of established resource-use patterns even after they are seen to be inimical to deeply cherished values. Ogburn (1922) touched many recurrent human experiences in speaking of "cultural lag."

FURTHER INQUIRIES

The writer is not altogether satisfied that low population density is a sufficient explanation for New Zealand's remarkable dedication of more than seven percent of its area to national park status. Further study is needed along the following lines:

(1) What historical circumstances have facilitated the political process of legislatively creating national parks? What experiences in the biographies of national park proponents have stimulated their efforts? What methods of advocacy did they employ, and which were most effective? What resistance was there? Specific attributes

of the land-classification controversy in the United States are replicated in New Zealand. In both countries, for example, there is lively competition between two land-management philosophies, and two government agencies exist which embody them. The New Zealand Forest Service, like its American counterpart, has come to use the phrase "multiple use" for invidiously comparing its programs with those of the National Parks Authority, to which it would have to yield jursdiction over certain lands upon which any new national parks might be created. Some New Zealand foresters view the United States as "the source of much emotional propaganda" fostering reallocation of land from Forest Service multiple-use management to "national parks devoted to a limited group of uses" (New Zealand Journal of Forestry, 1964: 119).

(2) How have New Zealand's location, characteristics, and history shaped a special New Zealand version of the national park concept? What special features of this concept have had transnational significance? For example, certain exotic fauna have been defined by law as "noxious" animals whose control by hunters is encouraged in the parks, partly as protection against deforestation and erosion. Hawaii, like New Zealand, has had problems with introduced species—for example, grass and goats.

(3) How does contact with natural environments and man-made facilities in national parks affect perceptions of and attitudes toward ecosystems and man's place in them? Do different categories of New Zealanders (such as rural versus urban, native-born versus immigrant, Maori versus Pakeha, high versus low education) differ on these points?

(4) How does New Zealand's remoteness from densely populated countries affect New Zealanders' attitudes toward ecosystems and man's place in them? How does the New Zealander's orientation toward Britain as "home" affect his assessment and evaluation of New Zealand's current and future population density? Does he conceive of an optimum or tolerable New Zealand population density near that of Britain? Does the extent to which he uses his national parks modify this in a downward direction? What changes in park management policies and practices do New Zealanders foresee as consequences of population growth (for example, curtailment of hunting in the parks as visitor density increases and makes hunting more hazardous to humans)?

(5) What family adaptations take place as families use the national parks? What age and sex patterns emerge in the division of labor and division of play in these environments? What forms of deviant or depreciative behavior occur in the parks? How are adult attitudes and values regarding national parks, natural environments, and appropriate behaviors therein, transmitted to children?

(6) What voluntary associations are park users affiliated with, and how do these influence visitor behavior and park management practices? How do they reflect competition between government agencies or other interests?

(7) How does human use of natural environments affect human use of man-made environments (cities)?

The basic intent of all these inquiries is to discover whether or to what extent wildland recreation helps foster ecological sophistication among those who engage in it and whether they acquire from it attitudes of "ecological humility." The writer assumes that such attitudes, and the discovery of ways of nurturing them, will ultimately contribute to human survival.

REFERENCES

Boulding, Kenneth E.
    1964 The Meaning of the Twentieth Century. New York: Harper & Row.
Carlson, Glen E.
    1943 "Human relations in forestry." Research Studies of the State College of Washington 12 (March 1944): 3-8.
Catton, William R., Jr.
    1965 "Intervening opportunities: barriers or stepping stones." Pacific Soc. Rev. 8 (Fall): 75-81.
    1969 "Motivations of wilderness users." Pulp and Paper Magazine of Canada (December 19): 121-126.
——— and Lennart Berggren
    1964 "Intervening opportunities and national park visitation rates." Pacific Soc. Rev. 7 (Fall): 66-73.
Cooley, Charles Horton
    1909 Social Organization. New York: Charles Scribner's.
Darling, F. Fraser and Noel D. Eichhorn
    1967 Man and Nature in the National Parks: Reflections on Policy. Washington, D.C.: Conservation Foundation.

Day, M. F.
    1962 "Preservation versus concentrated visitor use." Pp. 150-158
         in Alexander B. Adams (ed.) First World Conference on
         National Parks. Washington, D.C.: National Park Service,
         U.S. Department of the Interior.
Eddy, William H., Jr.
    1967 "Postscript." In D. F. Fraser and N. D. Eichhorn, Man and
         Nature in the National Parks: Reflections on Policy. Wash-
         ington, D.C.: Conservation Foundation.
Gilbert, Edmund W.
    1964 "Vaughan Cornish 1862-1948 and the advancement of
         knowledge relating to the beauty of scenery in town and
         country." Delivered to the Oxford Preservation Trust,
         Oxford, England, November 13.
Hardin, Garrett
    1968 "The tragedy of the commons." Science 162 (December
         13): 1243-1248.
Hendee, John C. and William R. Catton, Jr.
    1968 "Wilderness users: what do they think?" American Forests
         74 (September): 29-31, 60-61.
─── Larry D. Marlow, and C. Frank Brockman
    1968 "Wilderness users in the Pacific Northwest: their charac-
         teristics, values, and management preferences." USDA Forest
         Service Research Paper PNW-61. Portland, Ore.: Pacific
         Northwest Forest and Range Experiment Station.
Huizinga, Johan
    1950 Homo Ludens: A Study of the Play Element in Culture.
         Boston: Beacon.
Ise, John
    1961 Our National Park Policy: A Critical History. Baltimore:
         Johns Hopkins Press.
Klausner, Samuel Z.
    1969 "Recreation as social action." Appendix A in a Program for
         Outdoor Recreation Research. Washington, D.C.: National
         Academy of Sciences.
Leopold, Aldo
    1933 "The conservation ethic." Pp. 44-55 in Robert Disch (ed.)
         The Ecological Conscience: Values for Survival. Englewood
         Cliffs, N.J.: Prentice-Hall.
Linton, Ralph
    1936 The Study of Man. New York: Appleton-Century-Crofts.
Lucas, P. H. C.
    1970 Conserving New Zealand's Heritage. Wellington: A. R.
         Shearer, Government Printer.
McCaskill, Lance
    1965 "General aspects of recreation in national parks." New
         Zealand J. of Forestry 10: 155-157.

Mead, George Herbert
    1934   Mind, Self, and Society. Chicago: Univ. of Chicago Press.
National Academy of Sciences
    1969   A Program for Outdoor Recreation Research. Washington,
            D.C.
National Park Service
    1956   Mission 66: To Provide Adequate Protection and Develop-
            ment of the National Park System for Human Use. Wash-
            ington, D.C.: U.S. Department of the Interior (January).
National Parks of New Zealand
    1965   National Parks of New Zealand. Wellington: R. E. Owen,
            Government Printer.
New Zealand Journal of Forestry
    1964   "The recreational use of forest land." Editorial Note 9:
            119-121.
Nisbet, Robert A.
    1969   Social Change and History. New York: Oxford Univ. Press.
Ogburn, William F.
    1922   Social Change. New York: B. W. Huebsch.
Salmon, J. T.
    1960   Heritage Destroyed: The Crisis in Scenery Preservation in
            New Zealand. Wellington: A. H. and A. W. Reed.
Sutton, Ann and Myron Sutton
    1965   Guarding the Treasured Lands. Philadelphia: J. B. Lippin-
            cott.
Wisdom's Heritage
    1961   The National Parks of Canada. (Reprinted from the Annual
            Report of the Department of Northern Affairs and National
            Resources—fiscal year 1956-1957). Ottawa: Roger Duhamel,
            Queen's Printer and Controller of Stationery.
Working Party on National Parks Administration in New Zealand
    1966   Report. Wellington: Department of Lands and Survey
            (November).

SOCIOLOGY AND APPLIED
LEISURE RESEARCH

JOHN C. HENDEE
*Pacific Northwest Forest and Range
Experiment Station*

Leisure activity is not a social problem of the same magnitude as war, race, and poverty, but its importance is growing. Many people have not found satisfactory and fulfilling ways to utilize increasing amounts of leisure time. The prospect of more leisure to some unprepared segments of the population may not be appealing while those in the professions are working more than ever. And, as the outdoor recreation boom illustrates, the growth in leisure has led to unanticipated demands on natural resources that compete with other uses. A long list could be compiled illustrating leisure problem areas that have public or industrial policy needs to which sociological research might contribute.

Some recent task force deliberations reflect concern that the social sciences are not contributing as much to public policy and society as might be possible or desirable (Lyons, 1969; National Academy of Sciences-Social Research Council, 1970; National Science Foundation, 1969). The assumption is that a society with numerous growing social problems should find greater assistance from its sizable corps of social scientists. The social sciences, often described as emerging or in an embryonic stage, are relatively young when compared to the physical sciences, and this is often a valid explanation for comparatively meager applied contributions. Nevertheless, there is growing recognition of a gap between the promise and the fulfillment of expected contributions from social science (including sociology) to the solution of social problems (Robinson, 1967). Although theoretical, conceptual, and methodological tools may not yet be perfected, and information about human behavior and social institutions is not yet complete, sociology still has much to offer. Sociologists need to be more adequately challenged to exert greater effort to contribute relevant information from their field to social policy.

Some noteworthy problems plaguing attempts to increase leisure research concern the necessary financial support and conflict between applied and academic interests. Financing agents are interested in application, often to specific environments such as outdoor recreation settings, yet many competent scholars who might contribute have only theoretical interests. However, more than ever before, conceptual and theoretical development linked to application or conducted simultaneously with work leading to applied results are more salable in today's tight research money market. The future of leisure research may depend on the extent to which theory and conceptual development can ride the coattails of applied work, which is more easily funded.

For example, most competent sociologists are not likely to respond to public policy makers' and resource managers' requests for descriptive information describing clients and their preferences. Nor are administrators likely to respond to the sociologist's request for money in massive doses to do the "necessary theoretical research" that will presumably lead eventually to useful applied findings. Both perspectives have some merit. Policy makers in the leisure field need insights from good social research, but good sociologists are interested in developing theories which help explain social behavior, of which specific leisure behavior may be only a part. To the extent that theory and concepts are not developed, leisure data will fail to contribute understanding to human behavior in general, and specific interpretations and prediction to leisure settings will be limited as well.

The general shortage of data in a form useful to agencies focusing on application indicates that sociology has *not* demonstrated that investment in more basic theoretical research is a justified overhead cost and a successful strategy which develops the type of applied data desired by the funding agency (Weinberg, 1968). Research holding promise for immediate application, yet simultaneously wedded to the development of theory and method, offers an avenue toward financial support for sociological research that should be exploited. A tight research money market and the current state of the economy suggest a continued scarcity of dollars for work not tied to application and an increasingly competitive advantage for research proposals with well-developed application potential.

RESEARCH AS AN INVESTMENT

The trend is clear that public expenditures for research will be viewed more and more as investments to bring about or speed the attainment of social objectives. A growing rationality in budgeting techniques suggests that scarce resources should be allocated to diverse uses according to their importance. Science, in particular, with a relatively small political constituency, is justifiably dependent on rational arguments rather than on political pressure to support claims on public budgets (Shils, 1968). Pressures for efficiency and economy in the allocation of scarce resources led to development of the recent Planning, Program and Budgeting Techniques (Lyden and Miller, 1967). Although the survival of PPBS as a specific budgetary analytic technique may be uncertain, the concepts upon which it is based are certain to remain.

The challenge to leisure researchers and other would-be sociological entrepreneurs is to adapt their product to the current goal-oriented, cost-effective, budgeting criteria. For example, the allocation framework goes something like this. Given social objectives such as the constructive and satisfying use of increasing increments of leisure by growing segments of the public, how important is research in the sociology of leisure to obtaining such a goal relative to other public expenditure opportunities? Only by identifying the payoffs can research proposals meet such a criterion for choice.

Repugnant as this criterion may seem to academics, it governs new rules of the game. It calls for a different approach to planning and research priorities, and for new imaginative ways of evaluating and describing the impact and dividends of social research findings. Such criteria are particularly important to financing the future of leisure research, since established flows of money to sociology will be largely tied up in traditional fields of inquiry. The financial future of leisure research would thus seem to depend on its potential for application and the degree to which it can be sold on this basis.

RELEVANT LEISURE RESEARCH

The idea of conceptual and theoretical development in the field of leisure riding piggyback on applied social science is supplemented by the notion that new theories are not needed, since leisure behavior can be approached through established theoretical frameworks. Field and Burdge (1970: 4) point out that, "We are exploring an emerging major behavioral phenomenon which represents a reflection of society's development and change—namely, behavior in leisure and recreation—in which all existing sociological theory and methods must be employed." The integration of leisure activity with other behavior is further supported by Klausner (1969). He points out that, contrary to the traditional view of leisure as the purposeless counterpoint of work, leisure is far from purposeless when viewed within the context of the subgroups it serves, and, like work, it is directly tied to group goals and subject to obligatory norms. His proposal that recreation be analyzed in terms of a drama in which the players symbolically deal with a life problem is a promising approach further linking leisure activity to broader society and the mainstream of sociological research.

Integrated approaches such as the above, which link leisure to the rest of society, are easily adapted to current budgetary rationale. If recreation activity is a reflection of life problems for various society subgroups, then leisure research is tied to other social problems as well. For example, the recreation patterns of minority groups may reflect, more clearly than ever, their particular problems and the means of dealing with them. Likewise, middle-class leisure patterns may reflect the short-comings of their life styles and the tempo and trends of society. The additional public policy implications of broad, integrated approaches to leisure research are obvious, extending beyond the leisure setting to other segments of society. This added relevance should be used to support proposals for additional leisure research.

Some more directly applied questions also justify additional sociological study of leisure, yet provide the opportunity for a respectable scholarly approach. For example, given that public and private resources worth hundreds of millions of dollars are invested annually in recreational development, what are some of the noneconomic criteria that should guide such investments?[1] For example, if sociological study can identify the social meaning of recreation at a higher level of generalization than number of visits, dollars spent, and the like, what criteria might be developed to guide public investments in different types of recreation facilities to serve various social objectives? Surely there are sociological criteria for public resource allocations to the area of leisure that might more efficiently lead to the attainment of social goals or implicate undesirable goals that are perhaps unwittingly served by current allocations.

Likewise, a research investment framework justifies sociological research which attempts to identify and improve techniques for more accurately predicting future trends in the use of leisure time and demand for leisure-related facilities. For example, millions of dollars are spent periodically on predictive studies of outdoor recreation use that are consistently inaccurate, with predictions usually falling short of the participation realized. These predictive studies serve as a basis for the investment of millions of dollars by federal and state agencies. Clearly, more research is needed to identify crucial behavioral relationships and more accurate predictive techniques, and this basic effort might be supported by the promise of relevant application.

Similarly, existing sociological frameworks might be used to explore the recent proliferation and prominence of voluntary organizations in the conservation-leisure field, their political impact, and the necessary internal adaptations to a new balance of power by a host of affected public agencies and private industries. For example, the application of an instrumental-expressive framework (Jacoby and Babchuck, 1963) to conservation groups and outdoor clubs gives many insights into the activities of these voluntary organizations (Hendee et al., 1969).

In a recent call for more research on the social and behavioral dimensions of outdoor recreation, some additional problems were highlighted (National Academy of Sciences, 1969). They included: values implicit in current policy and allocation decisions; the patterns and benefits of leisure experiences in different locations to subgroups of the population; the career pattern of recreation participation, including recruitment, participation, and "dropout" rates for different activities viewed as analogs of questions familiar to occupational sociologists; therapeutic qualities of recreation experiences. Obviously, there is no shortage of leisure problems on which to do research. The problems cover a wide front familiar to established sociological interests and applicability to existing frameworks of inquiry. With some imagination, research proposals could be built around the relative dividends of new knowledge in these leisure areas.

Numerous other possibilities doubtlessly exist for leisure research to be justified by potential cost-effective contributions to application while simultaneously supporting the necessary conceptual and theoretical development. Yet the foregoing is fruitless if sociologists fail to include in their proposals provision for making their work applicable to the needs of the agency involved. Developing the policy implications of research is a task generally neglected by sociologists and a challenge to which they must respond in their search for relevance and increased financial support for leisure research.

It is a fact of life that administrators are not going to, nor should they, seek out policy implications in sociological journals. Unfortunately, although providing an appropriate environment for scholarly conceptual and theoretical work, academic sociology settings offer few internal incentives for applied, popular, or trade-level publication. On the contrary, sociological publication often seems designed only for sociologists—those in tune with the jargon and frameworks (Cheek and Rosenhaupt, 1968). This handicap to the use of sociological research findings might be partially overcome by joint ventures with professional schools having a vested interest in policy development and application. For example, university departments or colleges of forestry, physical education, parks and recreation, social work, education, and medicine have policy concerns and might willingly exploit the applied potential of sociological research findings to their fields. Such interdepartmental cooperation could provide insights into application possibilities for sociological research that would be useful in supporting proposals, as well as in freeing sociologists from unrewarded involvement in developing policy implications. Early collaboration during the research proposal stage would also help sociologists identify more accurately the applied potential to policy of their work in these fields.

CONCLUSION

The foregoing should not be construed as an argument for sociologists to prostitute their intellectual integrity to political ends and biased programs. Rather, it is an appeal for a relevant approach by sociologists interested in leisure so their growth may be supported by the usefulness of what they provide. This is particularly important to an emerging topic within a discipline. Whereas a "free scholar model" enables established divisions of a discipline to flourish (Wolfe, 1969), an emerging topic such as the sociology of leisure must challenge such forces if it is to attract financial support and talent for growth. Selling leisure research on the basis of its social utility could help do this. And, as I have argued, this need not detract from necessary conceptual and theoretical development if applied and academic efforts proceed together.

NOTE

1. A recent estimate of annual federal acquisition and capital improvement expenditures for outdoor recreation is $800 million (National Academy of Sciences, 1969).

REFERENCES

Cheek, Frances E. and Maureen Rosenhaupt
    1968 "Are sociologists incomprehensible? An objective study."
        Amer. J. of Sociology 73 (September/October): 617-627.
Field, Donald R. and Rabel J. Burdge
    1970 "Density and social interaction: a theoretical position for
        assessing participation standards in large recreation areas."
        Presented to the Rural Sociological Society, Washington,
        D.C.
Hendee, John C., Richard P. Gale, and Joseph Harry
    1969 "Conservation, politics, and democracy." J. of Soil and
        Water Conservation 24 (November/December): 212-215.
Jacoby, Arthur P. and Nicholas Babchuck
    1963 "Instrumental and expressive voluntary associations." Socio-
        logy and Social Research 47: 461-471.
Klausner, Samuel Z.
    1969 "Recreation as social action." Pp. 61-73 in a Program for
        Outdoor Recreation Research. Washington, D.C.: National
        Academy of Sciences.
Lyden, Fremont J. and Ernest G. Miller (eds.)
    1967 Planning Programming Budgeting: A Systems Approach to
        Management. Chicago: Markham.
Lyons, Gene Martin
    1969 The Uneasy Partnership: Social Science and the Federal
        Government in the 20th Century. New York: Russell Sage
        Foundation.

National Academy of Sciences
    1969 A Program for Outdoor Recreation Research. Washington,
         D.C.: National Academy of Sciences.
———-Social Science Research Council
    1970 The Behavioral and Social Sciences: Outlook and Needs. New
         York: Prentice-Hall.
National Science Foundation
    1969 "Knowledge into action: improving the nation's use of the
         social sciences." Report of the Special Commission on the
         Social Sciences of the National Science Board. Washington,
         D.C.
Robinson, James A.
    1967 "The case for a National Social Science Foundation." Pp.
         13-16 in The George Washington University Magazine,
         Washington, D.C.
Shils, Edward A. (ed.)
    1968 "Introduction." Pp. v-xiv in E. A. Shils (ed.) Criteria for
         Scientific Development: Public Policy and National Goals.
         Cambridge: MIT Press.
Weinberg, Alvin M.
    1968 "Criteria for scientific choice. II: the two cultures." Pp.
         80-89 in Edward A. Shils (ed.) Criteria for Scientific
         Development: Public Policy and National Goals. Cambridge:
         MIT Press.
Wolfe, Alan
    1969 "The myth of the free scholar." Center Magazine. Santa
         Barbara: Center for the Study of Democratic Institutions.